Silver Burdett Ginn Science

DISCOVERYWORKS

SCIENCE NOTEBOOK

Teacher Edition

GRADE 3

ACTIVITIES

UNIT PROJECTS

INVESTIGATE FURTHER

Silver Burdett Ginn
PARSIPPANY, NJ   NEEDHAM, MA
Atlanta, GA   Deerfield, IL   Irving, TX   Santa Clara, CA

CREDITS
Contributing artist
Mena Dolobowsky

Silver Burdett Ginn
A Division of Simon & Schuster
299 Jefferson Road, P.O. Box 480
Parsippany, NJ 07054-0480

ISBN 0-382-33747-6

4 5 6 7 8 9 10   H   05 04 03 02 01 00 99 98 97

CONTENTS

Name_____ Date_____

LIFE CYCLES
. . . .

In Unit A you'll learn about life cycles of animals and plants.
For the Unit Project, your group will make an Animal-Sitter's
and a Plant-Sitter's Guide and hold a classroom Book Fair.
Perhaps you already know something about taking care of
animals and plants.

Name all the kinds of animals you know that people have as
pets.

Students might name dogs, cats, horses, fish, birds, turtles, lizards, hermit crabs,
and so on.
_____
_____

What are some things that pets need?

Pets need food, water, and a clean, safe place to live.
_____
_____

Name some plants that people might have in their homes.

Students might name African violets, English ivy, cactus, philodendron, jade plant,
and so on.
_____
_____

What are some things that plants need?

Plants need light, water, soil, and protection from extreme temperatures and pests.
_____

Name _____ Date _____

UNIT PREVIEW
· ·

You probably know many things about plants and animals.
What are some more things you would like to learn? Make a
list of questions you have about plants and animals on the
lines below.

_____

_____

_____

_____

_____

_____

_____

_____

_____

_____

© Silver Burdett Ginn

Name_____ Date_____

LIFE CYCLES OF ANIMALS

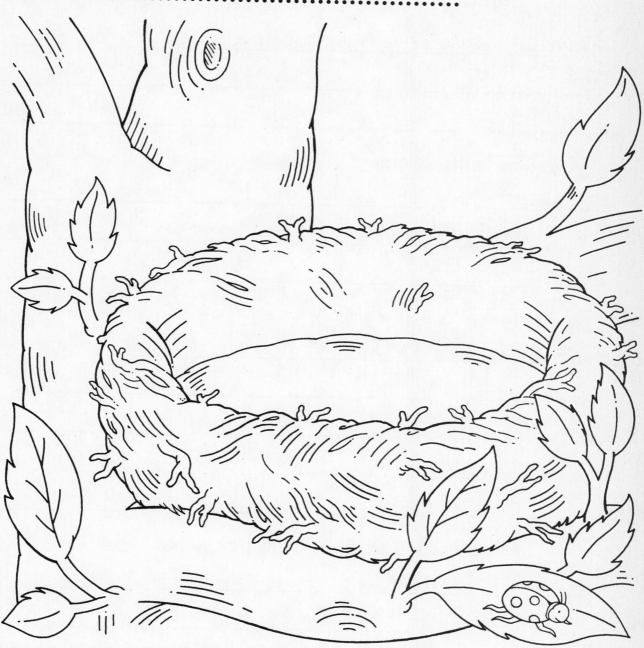

Students' drawings may vary. Some will show an adult bird sitting on eggs in the nest. Other students will show parent birds feeding or protecting the young birds.

You just found this empty bird's nest. Complete the picture to show how birds used the nest.

Name_____ Date_____

Dear Journal,

I think a life cycle is . . .

Some students may know that a life cycle is the ordered stages that occur in a plant's or animal's lifetime.

_____

_____

Some of the stages in the life cycle of an animal are . . .

Answers may vary. Many students will probably identify "baby" and "adult" as two stages. Some may know that an egg is the first stage in most animals' life cycles.

_____

_____

Some ways I've seen animals grow and develop are . . .

Answers will vary. Many students will probably describe little, awkward animals that grow larger, become more independent, and change features as they become adults.

_____

_____

_____

I've observed these things about animals caring for their young . . .

Many students will describe animal parents feeding and protecting their young.

_____

_____

_____

_____

ACTIVITY RECORD

CHAPTER 1

Name_____ Date_____

THE CHANGES CHART
· ·

Procedure

Record a list of living things that you've observed near your home or school.

Answers will vary but may include trees, shrubs, grass, birds, squirrels, dogs, butterflies, ants, and so on.

_____

_____

_____

_____

Write your prediction for how the plant or animal you chose for your Changes Chart will change as it gets older.

Answers will vary depending on what plant or animal students chose. In general, students should note that the plant or animal will get larger and may produce young of its own.

_____

_____

Analyze and Conclude

Write the answers to the questions in your book on the lines below.

1. Students' plans should include research or observation to check their predictions about the plant's or animal's life cycle.

_____

_____

_____

_____

Name_____ Date_____

2. Students should recognize where their predictions were accurate and where research or observations indicated that the life cycle was different from their predictions.

_____

_____

_____

INVESTIGATE FURTHER!

EXPERIMENT

Page A7

Explain your predictions for how you will change when you are 15, 25, and 55 years old.

Explanations will vary depending on their predictions. Many students will state that the changes are due to getting older, which causes the body to change.

INVESTIGATION CLOSE

Name_____ Date_____

  # INVESTIGATION 1
······································

1. Think about how a life cycle and a circle are alike. What must happen so that the life cycle of a species does not end?

   Reproduction is the way by which animals keep their species alive. At least some animals of a species must have babies, or there will be no young ones to grow up and produce the next generation. A species becomes extinct if the life cycle is broken.

   _____

   _____

   _____

2. Choose an animal and draw a picture of two different stages in its life. Order the stages by labeling them 1 and 2.

   Students' responses might include drawings of two stages in the life cycle of a butterfly, squirrel, duck, or frog. The drawings should number the stages in correct order.

CHAPTER **1**

ACTIVITY RECORD

Name_____ Date_____

BE "EGGS-ACT"!
∙∙∙∙∙∙∙∙∙∙∙∙∙∙∙∙∙∙∙∙∙∙∙∙∙∙∙∙∙∙∙∙∙∙

Procedure

Make a drawing from your memory
of the inside parts of an uncooked egg. Label
each part if you can. Mark the drawing *A*.

Students' drawings will vary, depending on what they remember. Most will show the yolk
and egg white.

Make a drawing of the outside of
the egg you observed.

Students should show the eggshell with pores.

Make a drawing of the inside parts
of the egg you observed. Mark this drawing *B*.

Students' drawings should show the yolk, egg white, shell lining and twisted strands of
lining, and possibly the white spot.

List the parts of an uncooked egg you showed in drawing *B* but
not in drawing *A*.

Answers may vary. Some students will list the shell lining, twisted strands of lining, and
the white spot.

© Silver Burdett Ginn

ACTIVITY RECORD

CHAPTER 1

Name_____ Date_____

Analyze and Conclude

Write the answers to the questions in your book on the lines below.

1. Students should hypothesize that all chicken eggs, and perhaps all bird eggs, have the same parts. They might suggest testing this hypothesis by observing eggs laid by other types of birds. Caution students not to disturb or break open bird eggs found in the wild.

_____

2. Students should infer that the shell of a chicken egg serves to protect the developing chick from attack, unclean or unhealthy conditions, or exposure to weather and climate changes.

_____

INVESTIGATE FURTHER!
⋯⋯⋯⋯⋯⋯⋯
EXPERIMENT

Page A13

What kind of eggs did you observe?

Students should name the animal from which the eggs came.

Tell how these eggs are different from chicken eggs.

Answers will vary depending on the kinds of eggs students observe. Some eggs may not have shells or shell linings. Most eggs will probably be smaller than a chicken egg.

Tell how these eggs are the same as chicken eggs.

Students' responses might include similarities in shape, color, and texture.

Name_____ Date_____

INVESTIGATE
FURTHER!
••••••••••••••••••
EXPERIMENT
Page A16

Describe your observations of the egg after it has been in water for 20 minutes.
Students should observe tiny air bubbles attached to the surface of the egg.

Explain how your observations prove there are pores in the eggshell.
The air bubbles had to come from inside the egg since there was no air flowing through the water.

Name_____ Date_____

INVESTIGATION 2

1. On page A15 you read about the parts of an egg. Think about each part and what it does. For each part, explain what would happen to the egg if that part didn't work.

If the shell did not form, there would be no place for the chick to grow. If the shell linings were missing, the air space could not form and the developing chick would die. Without the egg white, the chick could be bruised by the shell walls. Without the yolk, the chick would starve.

_____

_____

2. The first life-cycle stage is the same for animals that hatch and animals that are born live. Describe that stage.

In animals, the first life-cycle stage is an egg. Whether or not the egg produces a living animal depends on events and conditions, such as whether the egg is fertilized and adequately protected.

_____

_____

Draw what you think the inside of a chicken egg looks like just before the baby chick hatches.

Students should draw a fully formed baby chick inside the shell.

© Silver Burdett Ginn

CHAPTER 1

Name_____ Date_____

LOOK AT WHAT YOU'VE BECOME

Procedure

Write your prediction for what a mealworm needs to survive.

Mealworms need food, water, and a place to live.
_____

Which materials from the materials list meet each of the meal-worm's needs? Which materials provide water?

The dry cereal and slices of apple and potato provide food; the apple and potato also provide
water; the covered dish provides a place to live.

_____

Describe the home you made for the mealworm.

The mealworm's home is the covered dish with some dry cereal and slices of apple and
potato in it.

_____

Record any changes you observe in the mealworms over three weeks.

Day 1 _____Students should_____   Day 2 _____

Day 3 _____observe that the_____   Day 4 _____

Day 5 _____mealworms grow_____   Day 6 _____

Day 7 _____larger and change_____   Day 8 _____

Day 9 _____from worms to pupas_____   Day 10 _____

Day 11 _____to adult beetles._____   Day 12 _____

Day 13 _____   Day 14 _____

Day 15 _____

ACTIVITY RECORD

Name_____ Date_____

Analyze and Conclude

Write the answer to the question in your book on the lines below.

1. <u>Students should describe the changes mealworms went through as they matured into</u> <u>beetles: shedding their worm skins, becoming encased (pupa stage), and emerging as</u> <u>beetles.</u>

_____

Make your drawing in the space below.

2. Students' drawings should depict three stages of the beetle's life cycle that they observed: worm (larva), pupa, and beetle. Some students may infer that the life cycle also includes an egg stage.

INVESTIGATE
FURHER!
••••••••••••••••
EXPERIMENT

Page A21

Describe any changes you observe between the mealworm that is kept cold and the one that is at room temperature.

The mealworm kept cold eats less, moves more slowly, and changes at a slower rate than the one at room temperature.

Tell what you concluded about the effects of cold temperatures on a mealworm's life cycle.

Cold temperatures slow down a mealworm's life cycle.

Name_____ Date_____

THAT'S SOMETHING TO CHIRP ABOUT!
....

Procedure

Write your prediction for what a cricket needs in order to survive.

A cricket needs food, water, and a place to live.

_____

_____

Which materials from the materials list meet each of the cricket's needs? Which materials provide water?

The apple, lettuce, and cracker provide food; the apple and lettuce provide water; a terrarium with damp sand provides a place to live.

_____

_____

Record the day you first observe eggs in the egg chamber.

The day eggs are laid will vary._____

Record the day the eggs hatch.

The day eggs hatch will vary._____

Record your observations of how adult crickets and nymphs compare.

The nymph crickets are smaller than the adults and do not have fully developed wings.

_____

_____

ACTIVITY RECORD

CHAPTER 1

Name_____ Date_____

Analyze and Conclude

Write the answers to the questions in your book on the lines below.

1. Students may observe that nymphs are smaller and paler but generally have the same body shape as the adults. Unlike the nymphs, the adults have fully developed wings.

2. Students should identify the egg, nymph, and adult stages.

3. Students should recognize that the cricket's life cycle includes three stages, while the mealworm's life cycle (including the egg) has four stages. The cricket's body shape stays the same in the nymph and adult stages, while the mealworm's body changes.

INVESTIGATE FURTHER!
....
EXPERIMENT

Page A23

Record what happens to the nymphs as they grow.
As the nymphs grow, they shed their outer coverings several times.

Predict when the nymphs will become adults.
They are adults when they reach full size, have fully developed wings, and can reproduce.

Name_____ Date_____

INVESTIGATION 3
· ·

1. When a frog hatches from an egg, it has a tail that it later
loses. Then it looks like an adult. Tell whether the frog's life
cycle is complete or incomplete metamorphosis and explain why.

The metamorphosis of a frog is similar to complete metamorphosis however, accept
either answer as long as students can justify their reasoning.

_____

_____

2. Compare the life cycles of two animals—one that goes
through complete metamorphosis and one that goes through
incomplete metamorphosis.

Students may select different examples for each type of metamorphosis. For instance,
they may compare the life cycle of a butterfly (complete: egg, larva, pupa, adult) and a
cricket (incomplete: egg, nymph, adult).

_____

_____

Draw and label the life cycles of a mealworm and a cricket.

Students should show that the life cycle of a mealworm is complete metamorphosis with
four stages—egg, larva, pupa, and adult—and that the life cycle of a cricket is incomplete
metamorphosis with three stages—egg, nymph, and adult.

CHAPTER **1**

Name_____ Date_____

THE ANIMAL-SITTER'S GUIDE

Procedure

Record the name of the animal on the card you took from your group's animal-sitting assignment box.

Students should record the name of the animal printed on the card they chose.

Record what you find out about the baby animal's needs and how its parents care for it.

Answers will vary depending on the animal. In general, baby animals need food, water, a place to live, and protection. Not all animal babies are cared for by parents.

_____

_____

_____

_____

_____

_____

Write your inference about the care the baby animal should receive.

Students' inferences will vary depending on the animals they chose. In general, students should infer that the baby animals need food and water and a safe place to live.

_____

_____

_____

_____

Analyze and Conclude

Write the answers to the questions in your book on the lines below.

1. Students' responses might include obtaining food, providing adequate space, keeping the animal out of danger (for example, from a family pet), and maintaining necessary conditions, such as temperature and moisture.

_____

_____

_____

_____

2. Students should be able to defend their responses with logical explanations.

_____

_____

_____

_____

_____

_____

UNIT PROJECT LINK

Name_____ Date_____

UNIT PROJECT LINK
•••

In the space below, list all the different kinds of pets you can
think of. Beside the name of each kind of pet, try to write
the name of someone you know who has that kind of pet.

Students should list various kinds of pets, such as dog, cat, parakeet, goldfish, box
turtle, and so on. Beside the name of each pet, they should list the name of someone
they know who has that kind of pet.

_____

_____

_____

_____

_____

Which pets do you predict are hardest to care for? Explain why.

Answers will vary, but some students may think that larger pets, like horses, or exotic
pets, like monkeys, are hardest to care for.

_____

_____

Besides talking to pet owners, how could you find out about
the care of different pets?

Students could find out about pet care by talking to pet store owners or zoo keepers
or by reading pet-care books.

_____

_____

Share this information with your group.

Name_____ Date_____

INVESTIGATION 4

1. Think of a particular kind of very young animal. Suppose you found such an animal, and it was separated from its parents. Write how you might help care for the baby animal.

Students' responses should include the elements necessary for the young animal's survival,
such as food, safety, and the proper environment.

_____

_____

_____

2. Choose an animal you have learned about in this investigation. Describe the care that the animal gets as it grows and develops.

Responses should include information given in the investigation, such as how the animal
is born, what it is fed, where it lives, any threats to its safety and how it is protected,
and any training it receives from its parent.

_____

_____

_____

You read that a frog lays thousands of eggs. Draw what might happen to some of the eggs and tadpoles to keep them from becoming adults.

Students should show that many of the frog's eggs and tadpoles become food for other
animals, such as snakes and fish.

Name_____ Date_____

LIFE CYCLES OF ANIMALS

What is a life cycle?

A life cycle is the ordered stages that occur in a plant's or animal's lifetime.

_____

_____

What is the first stage in an animal's life cycle?

An egg is the first stage in the life cycle of almost all animals.

You learned how some animals grow and change. Name and describe two different kinds of life cycles.

Complete metamorphosis is a four-stage life cycle that has egg, larva, pupa, and adult stages. Incomplete metamorphosis is a three-stage life cycle that has egg, nymph, and adult stages.

_____

_____

_____

_____

How do animals care for their young?

Some animals, such as frogs, fish, and turtles, lay many eggs and let the young care for themselves. Other animals, such as birds and whales, feed and protect their young.

_____

_____

_____

_____

Name_____ Date_____

Think about what you learned in Chapter 1 when you answer the following questions.

1. Describe the most interesting thing you learned about the life cycles of animals.

Answers will vary. Accept all answers that describe a concept in the chapter.

_____

_____

_____

_____

2. What surprised you most about how animals grow and develop?

Answers will vary. Accept all answers that refer to the growth and development of animals.

_____

_____

_____

_____

3. What else would you like to learn about the life cycles of animals? How could you find out?

Answers will vary. Students may suggest using library resources, visiting a zoo or nature preserve, or talking to pet store owners, zoo keepers, or park naturalists to learn more about the life cycles of animals.

_____

_____

_____

© Silver Burdett Ginn

Name_____ Date_____

LIFE CYCLES OF PLANTS

Students' drawings should show the dande-lion going to seed, the seeds floating in the air and landing on the ground, the seeds sprouting, and the seedlings growing to mature, blooming plants.

A single dandelion is growing in the lawn. How will this dande-lion spread? Draw the stages in the life cycle of the dandelion to show how it can spread.

CHAPTER PREVIEW

Name_____ Date_____

Dear Journal,

Seeds are important to the life cycles of plants because . . .

They form new plants, which begin the life cycles over again.

_____

_____

Flowers are important to the life cycles of plants because . . .

They are where seeds are formed, which enable the life cycles of the plants to continue.

_____

_____

Some plants I know that produce cones are . . .

Answers may vary. Some cone-bearing plants are pines, spruces, cedars, firs, hemlocks, and redwoods.

_____

_____

Cones are important to the life cycles of plants because . . .

They form seeds, enabling the life cycles of the plants to continue.

_____

_____

Some things that plants need to survive are . . .

Answers may vary. Plants need air, sunlight, water, and protection from extreme temperatures and pests.

_____

_____

ACTIVITY RECORD

Name_____ Date_____

THE INSIDE STORY
....

Procedure

Make a drawing of your observations of the two halves of the lima bean seed. Draw arrows to each part of the seed. Number the arrows.

Students' drawings should show the seed coat, the stored food, and the embryo inside the lima bean seed. They should draw arrows to each of these parts.

Record the date you place the lima bean seeds inside the plastic bags.

Students should record the day, month, and year.

Record your observations of the bean seeds in the chart below.

Date	Observations
	Students should describe how the embryo grows and the stored food disappears.

CHAPTER 2

Name_____ Date_____

Analyze and Conclude

Write the answers to the questions in your book on the lines below.

1. Students should see the greatest embryo growth in whole seeds. The seed halves with the embryo should sprout. Nothing will sprout from the seed halves with no embryo. There must be an embryo and stored food (one or two seed halves) for a plant to grow.

_____

_____

_____

_____

2. Responses should reflect that students found three seed parts. Descriptions should include a covering (seed coat), the part that makes up most of the seed (stored food), and a tiny plant (embryo).

_____

_____

_____

3. Students should infer that the part that makes up most of the seed (the cotyledons, or stored food) provides food for the developing plant.

_____

_____

INVESTIGATION CLOSE

Name_____ Date_____

INVESTIGATION 1

1. In Chapter 1 you found out about the stages in the life cycles of animals. How is the seed stage in the life cycle of flowering plants like the egg stage in an animal's life cycle?

The seed is the first stage in the life cycle of flowering plants, and the egg is the first stage in the life cycle of an animal.

_____

_____

2. Explain how the parts of a seed help a flowering plant produce a new plant.

Students' responses should indicate that the seed coat protects the young plant and the stored food helps it begin to grow.

_____

_____

Draw a picture of one way seeds are scattered.

Students' drawings may show seeds being spread by wind, water, or animals.

© Silver Burdett Ginn

Name_____ Date_____

It's a Flower! It's a Factory!

Procedure

Make a drawing of the flower you examine. **Draw** an arrow to each part of the flower. Label any part that you know.

Students should draw the petals, pistil, and stamen of the flower they examine. Most students should be able to label the petals.

Make a drawing of the center part of the flower.

Students should draw the pistil with a swollen base and the stamens.

Record your questions about what you observed in the center of the flower.

Students' questions will vary. Some may ask what the parts in the center of the flower do.

_____

_____

_____

ACTIVITY RECORD

CHAPTER 2

Name_____ Date_____

Tell how your drawings of the flower compare with the photo in your book on page A45.

Students' drawings may vary depending on what kinds of flowers they observed; however, students' drawings should show petals, stamens, and a pistil.

_____

_____

Record your observations of how the pollen grains look and feel.

Generally, pollen grains look like tiny, yellow beads and feel like a sticky powder.

_____

Analyze and Conclude

Write the answers to the questions in your book on the lines below.

1. Students might suggest the center of a flower is a stable, strong place for insects to land. The seeds are also protected while they form.

_____

_____

2. Students might suggest that insects and birds get pollen on their body parts (legs, wings, beaks, heads) when visiting flowers. They then transport pollen from one flower to another.

_____

_____

3. Insects are attracted by the bright color of petals.

_____

_____

Name_____ Date_____

INVESTIGATION 2

1. Suppose you ordered a bowl of fruit at a restaurant. Your waiter delivers a bowl of sliced cucumbers. Was there a mistake? Explain your response.

Although cucumbers are generally considered vegetables, they are actually fruits, which contain and protect the seeds within them.

_____

_____

2. Describe the three main parts of a flower and tell how each part helps seeds form.

Students' responses should include that the stamen produces pollen, that the bright color of petals attracts birds and insects that carry pollen from a stamen to a pistil, and that the pistil is where seeds form.

_____

_____

Make a diagram to show the life cycle of a flowering plant.

Students' diagrams should include seeds, germination, growth and flower production, pollination, and seed formation.

Name_____ Date_____

CONE SWEET HOME

Procedure

Record your observations of the conifer cones.

Students should describe the scaly parts that make up the cones, as well as the size and color of the cones.

_____

Describe how you **classified** the cones.

Students' classifications will depend on what cones they examine. They should classify the cones by characteristics the cones share.

_____

Tell what kinds of conifers your cones come from.

Answers will depend on what kinds of cones students examine.

_____

_____

Make a drawing of what you observe on the cone scales.

Students should show a seed on the scale.

Analyze and Conclude

Write the answers to the questions in your book on the lines below.

1. Students might suggest that the job of a cone includes protecting the seeds and releasing the seeds when weather conditions are right.

_____

2. Responses should include that both cones and fruits protect seeds.

_____

Name_____ Date_____

INVESTIGATION 3
....

1. Think back to what you learned about flowering plants. What part of a conifer do you think is most like the fruit of a flowering plant? Explain your answer.

Students should explain that the cone of a conifer is most like the fruit of a flowering plant. The cone and fruit both protect seeds and are the site of seed production.

_____

_____

2. Describe how cones help make and protect seeds. Explain the role a cone can play in the regrowth that takes place following a forest fire.

Pollen cones make and release pollen. Seed cones receive the pollen and use it to make seeds. The scales of the seed cones help protect the seeds. Some cones need heat from a forest fire to release their seeds, thus encouraging forest regrowth.

_____

_____

Make a diagram of the life cycle of a conifer.

Students' diagrams should include seeds, a seedling, a mature tree with cones, pollination, and seed formation.

CHAPTER 2

Name_____ Date_____

SIZING UP TREE GROWTH

Procedure

Record your observations of the tree trunks in the two pictures on page A56.

The tree trunk grew bigger around as the tree got older.

_____

_____

Record your observations of the height of the lowest branch in each picture and the length of the branches in each picture.

The height of the lowest branch is the same in each picture. The same branches are longer on the mature tree than they are on the young tree.

_____

_____

Record your measurement of the distance around a tree trunk at a height of about 120 cm off the ground.

Students should record their measurements in centimeters.

_____

Based on your measurement, **estimate** the age of the tree.

Students can estimate the age by counting how many times a 2 1/2-cm strip of paper fits in their measurements.

_____

Record your observations of tree branches. Tell where color differences occur.

Students should observe that the branches are lighter or greener in color toward their tips.

_____

ACTIVITY RECORD

Use with pages A56–A57.

Name_____ Date_____

Analyze and Conclude

Write the answers to the questions in your book on the lines below.

1. Students should conclude that growth takes place at the tips of branches; the branches get longer and thicker.

_____

_____

2. Students should notice that a tree's trunk gets bigger around as it grows.

_____

_____

INVESTIGATE FURTHER!

RESEARCH

Page A57

Record your findings about how you can tell when a tree is sick or dying. List some changes caused by disease. Tell what might cause a tree to die.

Answers may vary. The leaves of sick or dying trees often look wilted and lighter than normal in color. The tree bark may be cracked and split. Drought, insects, and fungus are some causes of tree death.

Tell how you got your information.

Students might use encyclopedias or books about plants or talk to experts.

CHAPTER **2**

Name _____ Date _____

A CHANGE OF PLANTS

Procedure

Write your prediction about how each seedling will look in three days.

Seedling in the shoebox: ___Predictions may vary. Some students might predict that the seedling will bend and grow sideways to reach the light.___

_____

_____

Seedling hanging upside down: ___Predictions may vary. Some students might predict that the seedling will bend and grow upward.___

_____

_____

Seedling on a flat, lighted surface:

Predictions may vary. Some students might predict the seedling will grow upward in a normal way.

_____

_____

Record any changes you observe in each seedling after three days.

Seedling in the shoebox: ___Students should observe that the seedling is bent and growing sideways toward the light.___

_____

_____

Seedling hanging upside down: ___Students should observe that the seedling is bent and growing upward.___

_____

_____

Name _____ Date _____

Seedling on a flat, lighted surface: ___Students should observe that the seedling is___
growing upward in a normal way or it may be bending toward the light.

_____

_____

Analyze and Conclude

Write the answers to the questions in your book on the lines below.

1. ___Students should conclude that stems grow in the direction light is coming from and___
opposite the pull of gravity.

_____

_____

_____

_____

_____

2. __A plant might display inhibited growth or die.__

_____

_____

_____

UNIT
A

Name_____ Date_____

UNIT PROJECT LINK
· ·

Make a list of what you think the needs of plants are. How do
the needs of houseplants differ from those of outdoor plants?

Plants need air, light, water, protection from extreme temperatures and pests, and
sometimes fertilizer. Basically, the needs of houseplants and outdoor plants are the
same, though the specific needs of different kinds of plants may vary.

_____

Predict what might be some problems in caring for plants.

Predictions may vary. Some students might predict attack by pests and over- or under-
watering as problems.

_____

_____

Make a list of people you know whom you could talk with
about the problems of caring for plants and the solutions to
these problems.

Students should list relatives, friends, or neighbors who garden or have houseplants.

_____

_____

How else could you find out about solutions to problems in
caring for plants?

Students might suggest using library resources and talking to garden store workers
or local plant authorities.

_____

_____

Share this information with your group.

Name_____ Date_____

INVESTIGATION 4
....

1. Scientists have put experiments on the space shuttle to see how plants grow in a weightless environment. How would roots and stems be affected? Predict some problems in grow-ing seeds in space.

Students should realize that roots, which grow in the direction of the pull of gravity, and
stems, which grow opposite the direction of the pull of gravity, would be affected by the
lack of gravity in space. Students might predict that seeds might have difficulty sprouting.

_____

_____

_____

2. Explain one change in a plant's environment that can cause a growth change in the plant.

A possible response might be that a plant stem might change the direction it is turned
if the direction from which it receives light changes.

_____

_____

_____

Make a drawing of a plant that has an adaptation that helps to protect the plant.

Drawings will vary. Some students may draw plants with thorns or spines. Others may show
plants that are poisonous.

© Silver Burdett Ginn

Name_____ Date_____

LIFE CYCLES OF PLANTS

What is the first stage in the life cycle of a flowering plant?
Describe what this stage looks like.

A seed is the first stage in the life cycle of a plant. Inside the seed coat there is stored
food and an embryo.

_____

_____

How do flowering plants make seeds?

Seeds form in flowers inside the pistil after pollen from the stamen lands on the end of
the pistil.

_____

_____

_____

How do plants with cones make and protect seeds?

Pollen from pollen cones lands on seed cones where seeds are formed. Stiff, overlapping
scales protect the seeds.

_____

_____

How do plants change during their life cycles?

As plants get older, they get bigger and respond to light, water, and gravity by growing in
certain ways.

_____

_____

_____

CHAPTER WRAP-UP

Use with page A63.

Name_____ Date_____

Think about what you learned in Chapter 2 when you answer the following questions.

1. Describe the most interesting or surprising thing you learned about the life cycle of plants.

Answers will vary. Accept all answers that describe a concept in the chapter._____

_____

_____

_____

_____

2. The next time you see a flower, how will it remind you of the life cycle of plants?

Answers may vary. Students might recall that flowers produce seeds, which begin the

life cycle over again._____

_____

_____

_____

3. What else would you like to learn about the life cycles of plants? How could you find out about this?

Answers will vary. Students may suggest using library resources or talking to a plant

expert to learn more about the life cycles of plants._____

_____

_____

_____

Name_____ Date_____

LIFE CYCLES

Think about the Unit Project Big Event—the classroom Book
Fair—and about the Animal-Sitter's and Plant-Sitter's
Guides. How are the needs of animals and plants similar?
How are they different?

Plants and animals both need water, air, and protection from harmful things.
Animals need food, while plants need sunlight so they can make their own food.

_____

_____

_____

_____

How did the classroom Book Fair and Sitter's Guides help
you to prepare for caring for plants and animals?

Answers will vary. Students may site examples of procedures that they learned for
caring for specific plants and animals.

_____

_____

_____

What is the most helpful thing you learned about taking
care of plants or animals? Explain.

Answers will vary. Students should explain how they will put the information to use.

_____

_____

_____

_____

© Silver Burdett Ginn

UNIT
B

Name _____ Date _____

SUN, MOON, AND EARTH

In Unit B you'll learn about two of Earth's neighbors in space—the Moon and the Sun. You will also learn how Earth compares to these faraway bodies. For the Unit Project, your class will build a model Moon base. Think about what you already know about the Moon.

What do you think the Moon's surface looks like?

Answers may vary. Some students might know that the Moon's surface is covered
with craters and is made up of rocks and powdery gray soil.

_____

_____

_____

In what ways is the Moon's environment different from Earth's environment?

Answers may vary. Some students might know there is no air or water on the Moon
and there is less gravity than on Earth.

_____

_____

_____

How does the Moon move in space?

Answers may vary. Some students might know that the Moon revolves around Earth.

_____

_____

_____

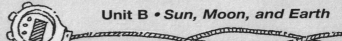

Name_____ Date_____

UNIT PREVIEW
....

What are some things you know about the Moon and the
Sun? What are some things you'd like to learn? Make a list
of questions on the lines below.

_____

_____

_____

_____

_____

_____

_____

_____

_____

_____

Name_____ Date_____

COMPARING SUN, MOON, AND EARTH

Here's an outline of the Moon. Draw in what you think its surface looks like.

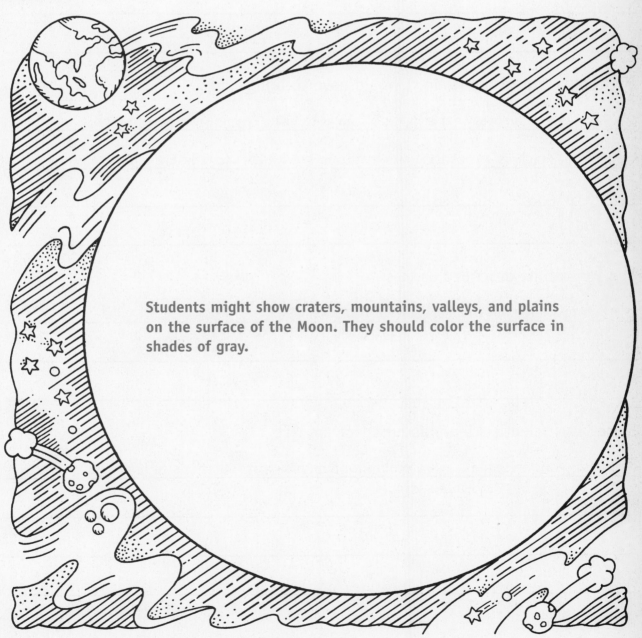

Students might show craters, mountains, valleys, and plains on the surface of the Moon. They should color the surface in shades of gray.

Name_____ Date_____

Dear Journal,

I think the Moon is different from Earth in these ways . . .

Students might suggest that the Moon is smaller than Earth and has no atmosphere, water,

or life. The Moon also has less gravity than Earth.

_____

_____

If I took a trip to the Moon, I would have to bring . . .

Students might suggest that they would have to bring oxygen, water, and food, as well as

something—such as a spacesuit—to maintain the proper air pressure and temperature.

_____

_____

The Sun can be described as . . .

The Sun is a huge, glowing ball of hot gases.

_____

_____

Some ways scientists learn about space are . . .

Scientists use telescopes, space probes, and human space missions to learn about space.

_____

_____

_____

CHAPTER 1

Name _____ Date _____

BIG EARTH, SMALL MOON

Procedure

Write your prediction about which object would be the right size to represent the Moon if Earth were the size of a globe.

Students' predictions will vary, depending on their understanding of the Earth-Moon size ratio and the objects they're comparing.

_____

_____

In the chart below, **record your measurements** of the distances around the objects.

Round Object	Distance Around the Object
Students should list each object they are given.	Students should record each object's circumference in centimeters.

Record how many Moon models it took to go across your model Earth.

It should take four Moon models.

CHAPTER 1

ACTIVITY RECORD

Name_____ Date_____

Analyze and Conclude

Write the answers to the questions in your book on the lines below.

1. Earth is about four times bigger across than the Moon. _____
_____

2. Students should choose the object whose string is about one-fourth the size of the globe's. Their decision should be based on their estimate of how much bigger Earth is than the Moon. _____

_____

INVESTIGATE FURTHER!
....
EXPERIMENT

Page B7

Measure and **record** how far you placed the object from the globe to represent the distance between the Moon and Earth.

Students' measurements will vary. The measurements should be written in centimeters.

Record the distance after you've measured nine and a half times around the globe.

Students' measurements will vary depending on the size of the globe. Measurements should be written in centimeters.

Compare the second measurement to your estimate.

Most estimates will be different from (either more or less than) the second measurement.

ACTIVITY RECORD

Name_____ Date_____

MAKING MOON CRATERS
• •

Procedure

Each time you drop the marble, **record** in the chart below the
height of the drop and the width of the crater.

Height of Drop	Width of Crater
25 cm 50 cm 75 cm 1 m	The width of craters may vary. Students should record measurements in centimeters.

Write a prediction about how the craters will compare when you
drop a large marble and a small marble from the same height.

Most students will probably predict that a larger marble creates a larger crater.

_____

_____

Record your results when you drop the large marble and the
small marble from the same height.

The crater produced by the large marble should be wider than the crater produced by the
small marble.

_____

_____

CHAPTER 1

ACTIVITY RECORD

Name_____ Date_____

Analyze and Conclude

Write the answers to the questions in your book on the lines below.

1. Students should observe that craters produced under similar conditions were about the same size.

_____

_____

2. Dropping a marble from a greater height will produce a larger crater.

_____

_____

3. The marble dropped from the greater height will move faster. This increase in speed causes a bigger crater to form.

_____

_____

4. Students should note that craters on the Moon are of various sizes. The craters were produced by objects of various sizes striking the Moon at various speeds.

_____

_____

Name_____ Date_____

UNIT PROJECT LINK

Look at a Moon map and choose a place you think would be good for a Moon base. Explain why you chose this place.

Answers will vary. Students should explain why they selected their sites, such as by describing a site as a flat area suitable for building.

_____

_____

Draw in the space below your first ideas about the design of your Moon base model.

Student designs should take into account the features of the place they've selected. Designs may be refined later as students learn more about conditions on the Moon.

Share this information with your group.

Name_____ Date_____

Describe how the newspaper print looks through
the water drops.
Students should note that the print looks enlarged.

Describe the shape of the drops. Are big drops and small
drops the same shape?
The drops have a curved, domelike surface. Big drops may spread out and be flatter.

How does the size of the drop affect how the printing
looks?
Small drops magnify the print more than large drops.

Infer why there is a difference in how the print looks with
small drops and large drops.
Small drops are more curved.

Name_____ Date_____

INVESTIGATION 1
....

1. Describe two ways in which the Moon differs from Earth.

The Moon is heavily cratered, has no atmosphere, and is about one-fourth the size of Earth. The Moon also lacks water and life—both of which are abundant on Earth.

_____

_____

2. Imagine that you took a walk on the Moon. Do you think your footprints would stay visible a long time? Or would they soon disappear? Explain your answer.

The footprints would remain visible for a very long time—perhaps indefinitely— because there is no wind or water on the Moon to erode the soil in which they were made.

_____

_____

Fill in the chart below with facts you've learned about the Moon.

MOON FACTS	
Distance across	3,476 km (2,160 mi)
Made of	gray rock
Atmosphere	none
High temperature	104°C (220°F)
Low temperature	-173°C (-279°F)
Distance from Earth	384,000 km (239,000 mi)

Name_____ Date_____

LUNAR OLYMPICS

Procedure

Record the measurement of the distance you can jump on Earth.

Students should record the distance between the two pieces of tape on the wall.

In the space below, **calculate** how high you could jump on the Moon.

Students should multiply the height they can jump on Earth by six.

Record the measurement of the weight of the book on Earth.

Students should record the weight of the book they measure using the bathroom scale.

In the space below, **multiply** the weight of the book by six.

Answers will vary depending on the weight of the book.

Analyze and Conclude

Write the answers to the questions in your book on the lines below.

1. Students might hypothesize that basketball, weight lifting, and track events such as the high jump, pole vault, and shot put would be fun because people could jump higher, lift more, and throw farther on the Moon. Students might hypothesize that the playing field or court would have to be bigger, the basketball hoop might be placed higher, special equipment for retrieving the basketballs might be needed, and so on.

2. There is less gravity on the Moon, so the performance of many athletic feats would be far easier than on Earth.

INVESTIGATE FURTHER

Name_____ Date_____

INVESTIGATE FURTHER!
....
EXPERIMENT

Page B19

Record the measurement of how far you can throw a ball on Earth.

Students should record the measurement of the distance they threw the ball.

Calculate how far you could throw a ball on the Moon.

Students should multiply the distance they threw the ball by 2.5.

Explain why the ball would go farther on the Moon.

Because there is less gravity on the Moon

CHAPTER 1

Name_____ Date_____

A MOON OUTING

Procedure

In the space below, **make two lists** of things you could and could not use on an outdoor picnic on the Moon.

Things I Could Use on the Moon

- baseball and bat
- flashlight
- playground slide
- playground swing
- shovel
- slingshot
- sunglasses
- umbrella
- yo-yo

Things I Could Not Use on the Moon

- bathing suit
- bicycle pump
- drums
- fan
- fishing pole
- insect repellent
- kite

In the space below, **make a list** of things you would need on the Moon. Explain why you would need each one.

Things I Would Need on the Moon   **Why I Would Need Them**

Answers may vary. Students should suggest water, oxygen, and food since there is no atmosphere on the Moon and an absence of water and living things. Many will also suggest spacesuits to provide the right temperature and air pressure, and radios to communicate.

ACTIVITY RECORD

Name _____ Date _____

Analyze and Conclude

Write the answers to the questions in your book on the lines below.

1. Because there is no water, air, or life on the Moon, items such as a bathing suit, bicycle pump, drums, fan, fishing pole, insect repellent, and kite are of no use there. (Students could use the umbrella as a Sun shield rather than for rain.)

_____

_____

_____

2. The lack of atmosphere and the weaker lunar gravity are the most important factors in determining which items to bring. Related to the lack of atmosphere is the absence of water and living things on the Moon.

_____

_____

_____

Name_____ Date_____

INVESTIGATION 2

1. Describe the conditions on the Moon that require astronauts to wear spacesuits.

The Moon has extreme temperatures, no atmosphere, and no water.

_____

_____

2. Explain why an astronaut on the Moon can carry something that weighs as much as the astronaut does.

Since the Moon's gravity is one-sixth that of Earth, the object would weigh only one-sixth of what it would weigh on Earth. The astronaut's muscles would be just as strong on the Moon as on Earth.

_____

Draw a cartoon in the space below to show how you might perform in a "Lunar Olympics" event of your choice.

Students' cartoons will vary, but should indicate the effects of the Moon's reduced gravity.

ACTIVITY RECORD

CHAPTER **1**

Name_____ Date_____

BIG STAR, SMALL EARTH

Procedure

Record the measurement of the width of your first circle model of Earth.

Students should record the width of their circles in centimeters.

_____

Record the measurement of the correct width for the model of Earth.

The correct width of the model of Earth should be 1/2 cm.

_____

Record the measurement of the distance you think there should be between the two models.

Students' estimates of distance between the two models will vary.

_____

In the space below, **calculate** the difference between the correct distance between the two models and the distance at which you placed them.

Answers will vary depending on students' estimates of distance between the two models.

Name_____ Date_____

Analyze and Conclude

Write the answers to the questions in your book on the lines below.

1. Students should infer that the Sun is more than 100 times wider than Earth—about 109 times larger in diameter.

2. Students should infer that the Sun is very, very far away from Earth, much farther away than the Moon is. In fact, the Sun is about 150 million km (93 million mi) from Earth.

INVESTIGATE
FURTHER!
• • • • • • • • • • • •
EXPERIMENT

Page B25

Record the measurement of how big your Moon model is.

Students' models of the Moon should be no larger than a tiny dot.

Record the measurement of how far away your Moon model is from the Earth model.

The models should be about 15 cm apart.

Check pages B11 and B13. How accurate are your estimates?

Answers will depend on students' estimates of the width of the Moon model and the distance from it to the Earth model.

Name_____ Date_____

MAKING SUNSPOTS
. . . .

Procedure

In the space below, **draw a picture** of your observations of the iron filings in the paper plate after the filings have been collected by the magnet.

Students should draw the patterns formed by the iron filings on the surface of the paper plate.

Analyze and Conclude

Write the answers to the questions in your book on the lines below.

1. The iron filings, like sunspots, form curved patterns around certain areas (the poles of the magnet in the activity).

_____

_____

2. Magnetic forces cause similar shapes to form in the iron filings and on the surface of the Sun.

_____

_____

Name_____ Date_____

INVESTIGATION 3
....

1. List several ways in which the Sun affects Earth.

Students might mention that the Sun warms Earth, provides light, and supplies energy for life on Earth. Solar storms cause the northern lights and southern lights and can also disturb the functioning of electrical equipment on Earth.

2. In the sky, the Sun and the Moon appear to be about the same size. Describe their real sizes compared with Earth's. Which of the two objects is farther away from Earth?

The Sun is much larger than Earth, while the Moon is about one-fourth the size of Earth. The Sun is much farther from Earth than the Moon is.

In the space below, make a drawing of the Sun's surface. Label the features of the Sun shown on your drawing.

Students' drawings should include sunspots, flares, and prominences.

CHAPTER WRAP-UP

Name_____ Date _____

COMPARING SUN, MOON, AND EARTH
....

What is the Moon like?

The Moon is a rocky body much smaller than Earth that has mountains, valleys, plains, and
craters. The Moon has no water or atmosphere and cannot support life.

_____

_____

How have scientists learned about the Moon?

Scientists have learned about the Moon by using telescopes, space probes, and human
space missions.

_____

_____

_____

What would it be like to be on the Moon?

Since there is no atmosphere, you'd have to carry oxygen and have a pressurized spacesuit.
You'd have to have water, food, and a heating and cooling system. Reduced gravity would
make it more difficult to get around until you became used to it.

_____

_____

What is the Sun like?

The Sun is a huge glowing ball of hot gases. Its surface has dark sunspots, bright flares,
and prominences.

_____

_____

CHAPTER WRAP-UP

Use with page B31.

Name_____ Date_____

Think about what you learned in Chapter 1 when you answer the
following questions.

1. What was something new you learned about the Moon?

Answers will vary. Accept any answers relating to concepts about the Moon covered in
the text.

_____

_____

2. After reading this chapter, would you be interested in visiting
the Moon? Explain your answer.

Answers will vary. Some students might be interested in visiting the Moon because of
the reduced gravity. Others may not be interested in visiting it because of the harsh
conditions.

_____

_____

3. What was the most surprising thing you learned about the Sun?

Answers will vary. Many students will be surprised that the Sun has magnetic storms
that affect things on Earth.

_____

_____

4. What is something else you would like to learn about the
Moon or Sun? How could you find out?

Answers will vary. Students might suggest looking at encyclopedias, reading books on
astronomy, visiting a museum, or talking to experts.

_____

_____

_____

Name_____ Date_____

MOTIONS OF EARTH AND THE MOON

Students should color in the Moons to represent phases of the Moon such as waxing crescent, first quarter, full, last quarter, waning crescent, and new. Some students may show gibbous Moons.

This night sky has six Moons! Color in each Moon to show how the shape of the Moon appears to change when you look at it at different times during a month.

CHAPTER PREVIEW

Use with pages B32–B33.

Name_____ Date_____

Dear Journal,

I think there is day and night on Earth because . . .

Earth rotates, or spins on its axis once every 24 hours. The parts of Earth facing the Sun have daytime, while the parts facing away from the Sun have nighttime.

_____

_____

_____

Two ways Earth moves in space are . . .

In addition to rotating, Earth revolves in an orbit around the Sun. This takes about 365 days.

_____

_____

The ways that the Moon moves in space are . . .

The Moon rotates on its axis and revolves around Earth about once a month. Some students may know that it takes the same amount of time (about 27 days) for the Moon to complete one revolution around Earth and one rotation, so that the same side of the Moon always faces Earth.

_____

_____

I think the Moon appears to change shape because . . .

The Moon appears to change shape because the Moon is lit by the Sun and revolves around Earth, so that people on Earth see different parts of the Moon's lit surface at different times.

_____

_____

_____

ACTIVITY RECORD

Name_____ Date_____

A SHADOW STICK SUNDIAL

Procedure

In the space below, **draw** a copy of your shadow stick sundial.
Add a little picture of the Sun to show where you had to put the
flashlight to re-create each shadow that you observed outside.
For each Sun picture, note whether you had to hold the flashlight
high or low.

Students' drawings may vary, depending on when they made their observations. The shortest shadow should be around noon and the longest shadows should be early and late in
the day. Students should draw a small picture of the Sun on the opposite side of the stick
from each shadow. They should include the four compass directions, with north being the
direction in which the shortest shadow points.

ACTIVITY RECORD

CHAPTER 2

Name_____ Date_____

Analyze and Conclude

Write the answers to the questions in your book on the lines below.

1. The Sun is low when the shadows are the longest._____

_____

2. Students should infer that the Sun appears to move from east to west._____

_____

_____

3. Students might hypothesize that the Sun revolves around Earth or that the Sun only *appears* to move because Earth itself rotates on an axis. Allow students to brainstorm and discuss different hypotheses before focusing in on Earth's rotation._____

_____

_____

ACTIVITY RECORD

Name_____ Date_____

MAKING A STAR CLOCK

Procedure

Draw the positions of the Big Dipper, Little Dipper, and Cassiopeia in the sky at 6:00 P.M. in mid-November. Show the star Polaris. Label your drawing 6:00 P.M.

Students should set their star clocks at 6:00 P.M. in mid-November and copy the positions of the Big Dipper, Little Dipper, and Cassiopeia from it.

Draw and label your predictions of how the Big Dipper, Little Dipper, Cassiopeia, and Polaris would look at 9:00 P.M. and 12:00 midnight on the same night in mid-November.

Students should show the star patterns moving in a counterclockwise circle around Polaris.

CHAPTER 2

ACTIVITY RECORD

Name_____ Date_____

Draw and label your predictions of how the Big Dipper, Little Dipper, Cassiopeia, and Polaris would look at 3:00 A.M. and 6:00 A.M. during the same night in mid-November.

Students should show the star patterns continuing in a counterclockwise circle around Polaris.

Analyze and Conclude

Write the answers to the questions in your book on the lines below.

1. Each star pattern appears to move in a counterclockwise circle around a fixed point in the northern sky.

_____

_____

_____

2. Students should note that Polaris remained in the same fixed position in the northern sky.

_____

ACTIVITY RECORD

Name_____ Date_____

3. Students should infer about 24 hours.

4. Students should infer that the stars appear to move across the sky at a regular pace so that with practice, people could tell time from the stars' positions.

5. After discussion, students should arrive at the hypothesis that the apparent movement of the stars is caused by the actual movement of Earth. This is the same sort of spinning motion, or rotation, that makes the Sun seem to move across the sky.

INVESTIGATE FURTHER!
•••••••••••••••••
EXPERIMENT

Page B37

Describe how you could use the star Polaris to help keep a ship on course.

Polaris always appears in the north. Knowing this, the other three directions can be inferred and a ship's course can be maintained.

Describe how Polaris would have helped Christopher Columbus find the Americas.

By knowing which way is north, Columbus could keep his ships on a westward course, which led him to the Americas.

Name_____ Date_____

 THINK IT WRITE IT

INVESTIGATION 1

• •

1. Describe how Earth moves during the course of a day.

<u>Students should mention that Earth rotates on its axis from west to east, making a</u>
<u>complete rotation every 24 hours.</u>

_____

_____

2. Just before you go to bed at night, you see a certain star in
the east. The next morning, just before dawn, you see the
same star in the west. Explain what happened to make the
star's position seem to change.

<u>As Earth turns, the stars seem to move across the sky. Because of the rotation of Earth</u>
<u>from west to east, stars that were in the east at bedtime would appear in the west</u>
<u>just before dawn.</u>

_____

_____

Make a labeled diagram to show why Polaris is always in the
same position in the night sky while other stars seem to move.

Students should show Polaris over Earth's North Pole and indicate Earth's rotation on its
axis, which points toward Polaris.

ACTIVITY RECORD

CHAPTER **2**

Name_____ Date_____

SUN PATHS
....

Procedure

Name the month in which the Sun appears highest in the sky.

June
_____

Name the month in which the Sun appears lowest in the sky.

December
_____

Name the month in which the Sun follows the longest path across the sky.

June
_____

Name the month in which the Sun follows the shortest path across the sky.

December
_____

Analyze and Conclude

Write the answers to the questions in your book on the lines below.

1. When the Sun appears highest and longest in the sky, the temperatures on Earth get warmer. When it appears lowest and for a shorter time in the sky, the temperatures are colder.

_____

2. June is hottest and December is coldest because the Sun is higher in the sky and visible longer in June, while in December it's lower and visible for a shorter time.

_____

_____

Name_____ Date_____

3. The four months would not all have the same amount of daylight. June has the longest day because the Sun's path is longest in June. December has the shortest day because the Sun's path is shortest in December.

_____

_____

4. Earth's daily rotation does not explain why the Sun's path would change during the year. This activity suggests that something else is happening on a yearly basis. Students might hypothesize that Earth's movement around the Sun causes the changes shown in the pictures.

_____

_____

Name_____ Date_____

CONSTELLATIONS THROUGH THE YEAR

Procedure

Draw a picture of the Sun and the constellations Leo, Scorpius, Pegasus, and Orion as if you were looking down on the scene from above. Draw Earth where it would have to be to see the constellation Leo. Label the parts of the drawing and title the whole drawing *spring*.

Students should draw the Sun in the center and the constellations in an outer ring, with Leo at 12 o'clock, Orion at 3 o'clock, Pegasus at 6 o'clock, and Scorpius at 9 o'clock. Earth should be between the Sun and Leo.

Draw a picture of the Sun and constellations as you did above. Show where Earth would have to be to see Scorpius. Title this drawing *summer*.

Students should show Earth between the Sun and Scorpius.

Name_____ Date_____

Draw a picture of the Sun and constellations as you did on page 75. Show where Earth would have to be to see Pegasus. Title this drawing *autumn*.

Students should show Earth between the Sun and Pegasus.

Draw a picture of the Sun and constellations as you did above. This time show Earth where it would have to be to see Orion. Title this drawing *winter*.

Students should show Earth between the Sun and Orion.

ACTIVITY RECORD

Name_____ Date_____

Analyze and Conclude

Write the answers to the questions in your book on the lines below.

1. Earth moves around the Sun along a path that resembles a circle._____
_____

2. Different constellations are visible in different seasons because Earth's position relative to the Sun changes throughout the year. The night side of Earth thus faces in different directions at different times of the year._____
_____

INVESTIGATE FURTHER!
....
RESEARCH
Page B45

Explain where the names of the constellations Leo, Scorpius, Pegasus, and Orion come from and what each means.

The names come from ancient Greek mythology. Leo is a lion; Scorpius is a scorpion whose sting killed Orion the hunter; and Pegasus is a winged horse.

Record which constellation or constellations you could see in the night sky.

Answers will vary depending on the season in which students observe the sky and from where they observe it.

Name_____ Date_____

INVESTIGATION 2

1. Describe how Earth moves during the course of a year. Why is a year about 365 days long?

<u>Earth revolves around the Sun during a year. It takes about 365 days to complete one</u>
<u>revolution.</u>

_____

_____

2. Explain why the constellation named Taurus the Bull is visible in November but not in May.

<u>Because of Earth's yearly orbit around the Sun, some constellations are visible in the</u>
<u>night sky during some times of the year but not at other times. Taurus is visible in</u>
<u>November because the night side of Earth faces Taurus at that time of the year. In May,</u>
<u>Earth is on the other side of the Sun from Taurus. So only the day side of Earth faces</u>
<u>that constellation in May.</u>

_____

_____

Make a labeled diagram to show two ways Earth moves in space.

Students' diagrams should indicate that Earth rotates on its axis and revolves around the Sun.

Name_____ Date_____

MOON PHASER

Procedure

Make a drawing to show the positions of the Moon model, the Sun model, and your head when the Moon model looks to you like picture *A*. The scene should be drawn as if you were looking down on it from the ceiling. Label all the objects you draw and title the drawing *A*.

Students should show the Moon between the Sun and Earth and to one side, so that the three bodies form about a 45° angle. The lit sides of Earth and the Moon should face the Sun.

Make a drawing like the one above to show when the Moon model looks like picture *B*. Title this drawing *B*.

Students should show the Sun, Earth, and the Moon forming a right angle with the Moon to one side of Earth. The lit sides of Earth and the Moon should face the Sun, with the Moon having moved a short distance in a counterclockwise direction since picture *A*.

Name_____ Date_____

Make a drawing like the ones on page 79 to show when the Moon model looks like picture *C*. Title this drawing *C*.

Students should show the Sun, Earth, and Moon in a straight line in that order.

Make a drawing to show when the Moon model looks like picture *D*. Title the drawing *D*.

Students should show the Sun, Earth, and Moon forming a right angle, with the Moon on the opposite side of Earth from picture *B*.

Make a drawing to show when the Moon model looks like picture *E*. Title this drawing *E*.

Students should show the Sun, Moon, and Earth forming about a 45° angle, with the Moon on the other side of Earth from picture *A*.

ACTIVITY RECORD

CHAPTER 2

Name_____ Date_____

Make a drawing to show when the Moon model looks like picture *F*.
Title this drawing *F*.

Students should show the Sun, Moon, and Earth in a straight line in that order.

Analyze and Conclude

Write the answers to the questions in your book on the lines below.

1. Students should identify the object they represent as Earth.
_____

2. Students should infer that the Moon revolves around Earth.
_____

Name_____ Date_____

UNIT PROJECT LINK
....

Describe what happens to the Moon base on the Moon
model as you re-create each picture on page B51.

Picture *A* _Students' descriptions will depend_

Picture *B* _on where they locate the Moon base_

Picture *C* _on the Moon model. They should tell_

Picture *D* _when it is night and day at the Moon_

Picture *E* _base._

Picture *F* _____

Infer what the days and nights would be like at your Moon
base.

Students should infer the Moon base will spend about half its time in sunlight and
half in darkness as the Moon revolves around Earth. Days and nights on the Moon are
each about two weeks long.

_____

_____

Explain how the things you learned in this activity will
affect your plans for the Moon base.

Answers may vary. Students might relate the long periods of sunlight and darkness
to the need for cooling and heating and lighting at the Moon base.

_____

_____

Share this information with your group.

INVESTIGATION CLOSE

Name _____ Date _____

INVESTIGATION 3

1. Describe how the motions of the Moon cause its phases.

We see the same half of the Moon from Earth all the time. As the Moon revolves around Earth, however, different portions of the Moon are lit by the Sun. The amount of the lit portion of the Moon that we can see from Earth determines the Moon's phase.

2. Is it correct to call the far side of the Moon the dark side? Why or why not?

The far side of the Moon is only the dark side during a full Moon, when none of the far side is lit by the Sun. At other times, some or all of the far side is lit.

Make a labeled diagram to show two ways the Moon moves in space.

Students' diagrams should indicate that the Moon rotates on its axis and revolves around Earth, with the same side of the Moon always facing Earth.

Name_____ Date_____

MOTIONS OF EARTH AND THE MOON

Explain how Earth moves each day.

Earth rotates, or spins on its axis, one complete turn every 24 hours, or day.

_____

_____

How does Earth move throughout the year?

Earth makes one complete revolution in its orbit around the Sun in about 365 days, or one year.

_____

_____

Compare Ptolemy's ideas about the Sun and Earth with the ideas of Copernicus. Whose ideas proved to be true?

Ptolemy hypothesized that the Sun and other objects in the sky revolved around an unmoving Earth. Copernicus thought the Sun was at the center of the solar system and Earth and other planets revolved around it, which we know now to be true.

_____

_____

How does the Moon move?

The Moon rotates on its axis about once a month (every 27 days) and revolves around Earth in the same period of time.

_____

_____

CHAPTER WRAP-UP

Use with page B57.

Name_____ Date_____

Think about what you learned in Chapter 2 when you answer the following questions.

1. How will you think about a rising and setting Sun now that you know how Earth moves?

The Sun is not moving through the sky. It only appears to do so as Earth rotates.

_____

_____

2. Look again at the shapes of the Moon you colored on page 65. How would you change them now that you know about the phases of the Moon?

Answers will vary. Students might suggest reordering their drawings or adding some different phases they left out.

_____

_____

3. What was the most interesting thing you learned in this chapter? Explain your answer.

Answers will vary. Some students might say the fact that the same side of the Moon always faces Earth was the most interesting since this phenomenon creates mystery about the far side of the Moon.

_____

_____

4. Is there anything about how Earth or the Moon moves that you're still not sure about? How can you find out?

Answers will vary. Students might suggest rereading the chapter, looking in other books on astronomy, or asking questions.

_____

_____

Name_____ Date_____

EFFECTS OF EARTH AND MOON MOTIONS

Complete this picture to show your favorite season of the year.

Students should add details to the scene pictured to make it appear as spring, summer, fall, or winter.

Name_____ Date_____

Dear Journal,

I think that some parts of the year are hotter and some parts are colder because . . .

Answers may vary. Some students might suggest that the Sun seems hotter and shines longer during some parts of the year than during other parts. Some might infer that the Sun's rays strike places on Earth at different angles at different times of the year, making it hotter or colder.

_____

_____

_____

I think there are different seasons in a year because . . .

Answers may vary. Some students might know that seasons are caused by the tilt of Earth's axis and its orbit around the Sun, which result in the Sun's rays striking each place on Earth differently at different times of the year.

_____

_____

_____

I think that an eclipse is . . .

Students might suggest that an eclipse is when the Sun or Moon seems to disappear.

_____

_____

_____

An eclipse is caused by . . .

Some students might know that an eclipse is caused by either the Moon or Earth blocking the Sun's light and occurs when the Sun, Moon, and Earth line up in a straight line.

_____

_____

Name_____ Date_____

LINED-PAPER SUNLIGHT

Procedure

In the space below, **draw a picture** to show how the rays of sunlight strike different parts of your model Earth.

Students should show the rays closest together and vertical as they strike the equator and farthest apart and most slanted as they strike the two poles.

Draw a picture to show how the rays of sunlight strike different parts of your model Earth after you turn the model so that the North Pole is tilted to the right.

Students should show the rays closest together and vertical as they strike just south of the equator and farthest apart and most slanted as they strike to the left of the North Pole and to the right of the South Pole.

ACTIVITY RECORD

Name_____ Date_____

Analyze and Conclude

Write the answers to the questions in your book on the lines below.

1. The area where the rays are closest together and vertical when they hit the ground is at the equator in step 4 and just south of the equator in step 5. The area where the rays are farthest apart and most slanted is at the two poles in step 4; it is to the left of the North Pole and just right of the South Pole in step 5.

_____

_____

2. The closer the rays in the model, the warmer the temperature. The more directly the real Sun's rays hit, the warmer it is. The more slanted they hit, the cooler it is.

_____

_____

3. It would be hottest at the equator in step 4 and just south of the equator in step 5. It would be coldest at both poles in step 4 and where the rays never hit at the North Pole in step 5.

_____

ACTIVITY RECORD

CHAPTER 3

Name_____ Date_____

EARTH TILTS!

Procedure

Record your observations of which parts of your model Earth are getting the most sunlight when you first point the North Pole toward the Polaris drawing.

Answers will vary depending on where students are holding their Earth models in relation to the "Sun."

Record your observations of which parts of your Earth model get the most sunlight at each of the four points shown in the picture on page B63.

Students should identify the parts of the model tilted toward the "Sun" as getting the most sunlight.

Analyze and Conclude

Write the answers to the questions in your book on the lines below.

1. A state in North America will get the most sunlight when the North Pole is tilted toward the Sun and the least sunlight when the North Pole is tilted away from the Sun.

2. The seasons in the Northern Hemisphere occur when the North Pole is in the following positions: tilted toward the Sun in summer; tilted away from the Sun in winter; tilted neither toward nor away from the Sun in spring and autumn. Make sure students have the seasons in the correct order with the globe orbiting counterclockwise.

Name_____ Date_____

UNIT PROJECT LINK

In the space below, draw a sketch of a sky scene that you would like to make for your Moon base model. Label the Sun, Earth, and stars.

Students' sketches will vary. Earth should appear as a fairly large object in the sky, while the Sun and other stars will appear much the same as they do from Earth, but they'll be visible at the same time in a black sky.

How will you show the day and night parts of Earth in your scene?

Answers will vary. Most students will suggest making the day part of Earth in brighter colors than the night parts. The day part of Earth should face the Sun.
_____

How will you show the tilt of Earth's axis in your scene?

Answers will vary. Students might suggest having either the North or South Pole tilted away from view.
_____

How could you tell what season it is in the United States in your scene?

Students can determine the season by by observation Earth is tilted in relation to the Sun and whether the U.S. is receiving direct or indirect sunlight.
_____

Share this information with your group.

INVESTIGATE FURTHER

Name_____ Date_____

INVESTIGATE
FURTHER!
....
RESEARCH

Page B66

List your examples of how people in different countries celebrate the changing seasons.

Examples will vary depending on the cultures and countries students research.

Record the sources you used for your research.

Possible resources include encyclopedias, books on various countries and cultures, and discussions with people from different cultures and countries.

Share your examples with your classmates.

Name_____ Date_____

INVESTIGATION 1
·····································

1. Explain how Earth's movements cause the four seasons.

Earth always tilts in the same direction as it revolves around the Sun. Because of this tilt, the Sun's rays fall on particular parts of Earth at different angles at different times of the year. This change in the amount of sunlight results in seasons.

_____

_____

2. Suppose you're planning an expedition to the South Pole. What month would you choose to visit there? Explain the reasons for your choice. Describe the conditions you'd expect to find then.

Students might plan a visit in December or January because that is when the South Pole begins its warmest season and has its longest days. Accept all responses supported by reasonable explanations and accurate descriptions of seasonal conditions.

_____

Draw a labeled diagram to show why it is always hotter near the equator.

Students' diagrams may vary, but they should indicate that no matter how Earth is tilted, the equator always receives the most direct rays of sunlight.

© Silver Burdett Ginn

ACTIVITY RECORD

Name_____ Date_____

A DISAPPEARING ACT

Procedure

Describe your observations of each stage of the solar eclipse shown in the photograph on page B73.

Students' descriptions may vary. They should note that larger portions of the Sun appear dark until the entire Sun appears dark in the middle stage; then the dark portion shrinks again. They should note that a bright haze appears around the Sun in the middle photo.

_____

_____

Describe your observations of each stage of the lunar eclipse shown in the photograph on page B73.

Students' descriptions may vary. They should note that larger portions of the Moon appear dark until the entire Moon appears dark—in fact, reddish—in the middle stage; then the dark portion shrinks again.

_____

_____

Record your description of any differences you observe between a solar eclipse and a lunar eclipse.

Students might note that in a solar eclipse, the Sun becomes completely black with a bright haze around the edges; in a lunar eclipse, the Moon remains faintly visible and turns reddish. They may also note that the dark portions appear on different sides in the two eclipses.

_____

_____

Name_____ Date_____

Analyze and Conclude

Write the answers to the questions in your book on the lines below.

1. A solar eclipse occurs when the Moon passes between the Sun and Earth and blocks our view of the Sun.

_____

_____

2. A lunar eclipse occurs when the Moon moves into Earth's shadow.

_____

_____

Name_____ Date_____

HOMEMADE ECLIPSES

Procedure

In the space below, **make a drawing** of the solar eclipse you modeled using a lamp, a plastic-foam ball, and yourself. Label the Sun, Earth, and the Moon on your drawing and title it *Solar Eclipse*.

Students should show the Moon directly between the Sun and Earth.

Make a drawing of the lunar eclipse you modeled using a lamp, a plastic-foam ball, and a globe. Label the drawing and title it *Lunar Eclipse*.

Students should show Earth directly between the Sun and Moon.

ACTIVITY RECORD

Name_____ Date_____

Analyze and Conclude

Write the answers to the questions in your book on the lines below.

1. In a solar eclipse, the Moon is between the Sun and Earth, so that it blocks the Sun from our view.

_____

_____

2. During a solar eclipse, the Moon's phase is a new Moon.

_____

3. In a lunar eclipse, Earth is between the Sun and the Moon, so that the Moon is in Earth's shadow.

_____

_____

4. During a lunar eclipse, the Moon's phase is a full Moon.

_____

_____

INVESTIGATE FURTHER

Name_____ Date_____

INVESTIGATE
FURTHER!
....
EXPERIMENT
Page B75

Describe the results of your experiments with the lamp, globe, and Moon model to create solar and lunar eclipses.

Students should note that eclipses occur only when the Sun, Moon, and Earth line up exactly right.

Compare the positions of the Sun, Moon, and Earth that produce eclipses with the positions that produce a full and new Moon.

A lunar eclipse occurs only when the Moon is full and the Sun, Earth, and Moon are exactly aligned. A solar eclipse occurs only when the Moon is new and the Sun, Moon, and Earth are exactly aligned.

Infer why we don't see solar and lunar eclipses every month.

Because the Moon's orbit around Earth tilts a little, so the Moon is usually above or below the positions that would produce eclipses.

© Silver Burdett Ginn

Name_____ Date_____

INVESTIGATION 2

1. Describe the positions of the Sun, Earth, and the Moon during a solar eclipse. Do the same thing for a lunar eclipse.

During a solar eclipse, the Moon is directly between the Sun and Earth. During a lunar eclipse, Earth is directly between the Sun and the Moon.

_____

_____

_____

2. In a solar eclipse, what object casts a shadow on what other object? Explain what this shadow has to do with the fact that each solar eclipse is only visible from certain areas on Earth.

The Moon casts a shadow on Earth during a solar eclipse. Since the Moon's shadow is not large enough to cover all of Earth, the eclipse is only visible from the part of Earth touched by the Moon's shadow.

_____

Draw a labeled diagram to show the positions of the Sun, Earth, and the Moon during a total solar eclipse that can be seen where you live.

Students should show the Sun, the Moon, and Earth in that order, exactly aligned so that the point where students live lines up directly with the Moon and Sun and the Moon's shadow falls at the spot when students live.

Name_____ Date_____

EFFECTS OF EARTH AND MOON MOTIONS

What causes seasons to occur on Earth?

The tilt of Earth's axis causes seasons because the Sun's rays strike each place on Earth differently at different times of the year as Earth revolves in its orbit.

Compare how the Sun's rays strike Earth at the equator and at the poles.

The equator receives the most direct rays from the Sun year round, while the poles receive the most indirect rays. When it is winter in the Northern Hemisphere, the North Pole tilts away from the Sun and is in darkness while the South Pole tilts toward the Sun and receives nonstop sunlight. This situation reverses when it is summer in the Northern Hemisphere and winter in the Southern Hemisphere.

What is an eclipse? Name two kinds of eclipses.

An eclipse is when the Sun or Moon appears to disappear. The two kinds of eclipses are a solar eclipse and lunar eclipse.

Compare the two kinds of eclipses.

During a solar eclipse, the Moon passes between the Sun and Earth. During a lunar eclipse, the Moon passes into Earth's shadow.

CHAPTER WRAP-UP

Use with page B79.

Name_____ Date_____

Think about what you learned in Chapter 3 when you answer the following questions.

1. How does what you learned change the way you think about seasons?

Answers may vary. Students might suggest relating the tilt of Earth's axis and its orbit around the Sun to the seasons.

_____

_____

_____

2. How does what you learned help you understand the climate in different parts of the world?

Students might mention how Earth's roundness and its tilt on its axis affects how much sunlight different parts of Earth receive, which affects climate.

_____

_____

_____

3. How did learning about eclipses help you to better understand Earth's and the Moon's movements?

Answers may vary. Eclipses are dramatic visible evidence of the Moon's movement and point out that the positions of Earth and the Moon are constantly changing in relation to each other and to the Sun.

_____

_____

_____

Name_____ Date_____

UNIT PROJECT WRAP-UP

Think about your Moon base model and the story you created about what life might be like on a Moon base. What do you think the most realistic part of your model is? Explain your answer.

Answers will vary. Students should identify a part of the Moon base model and tell why they think it is the most realistic.

_____

_____

What part of your Moon base model do you think could be improved? Explain how it could be improved.

Answers will vary. Students should describe a part of the Moon base model and tell how it could be made better.

_____

_____

How do you think your Moon base model and story helped others learn about the Moon?

Answers will vary. Students might state that the model and story helped others learn about the characteristics of the Moon, such as the lack of atmosphere, water, or living things and the difference in gravity compared to Earth.

_____

_____

How did making your Moon base model and creating your story help you learn more about the Moon?

Answers will vary. Some students might suggest that doing this project made them more aware of the differences between Earth and the Moon and made them relaize how difficult it would be to live on the Moon.

_____

UNIT
C

Name_____ Date_____

FORMS OF ENERGY

In Unit C you'll learn about energy, its different forms, and how to save it. For the Unit Project Big Event, you'll design and build an energy-efficient model home. You'll test the energy efficiency of your model home by timing how long it takes an ice cube to melt inside the house.

What is energy?

The ability to move something or cause a change in matter

_____

What forms of energy do you think are used in a house?

Students might mention electrical, mechanical, solar, heat, light, and chemical.

_____

How is energy used in a home?

Possible answers include heating the home, cooling it, lighting the house, using
appliances, opening the garage door, and mowing the lawn.

_____

_____

List some ways you could save energy in the home.

Possible answers include turning off lights and appliances when not using them,
using fans instead of air conditioning, lowering the thermostat in winter, and adding
insulation to the home.

_____

UNIT C

Name_____ Date_____

UNIT PREVIEW

What do you already know about forms of energy? What would you like to learn? Make a list of questions you have about energy on the lines below.

_____

_____

_____

_____

_____

_____

_____

_____

_____

_____

_____

Name_____ Date_____

ENERGY
....

Think about all the things at an amusement park. Draw some things that are using energy.

Students' drawings will vary. Most students will draw moving amusement rides.

Name_____ Date_____

Dear Journal,

I think that energy is . . .

<u>Some students might know that energy is the ability to move things or to cause a change</u>
<u>in matter.</u>

_____

_____

_____

I use energy when I do these things . . .

<u>Possible answers include move, eat, talk, breathe, ride a bike, turn on a light, play ball,</u>
<u>turn on the TV, play a game, and ride in a car.</u>

_____

_____

_____

Energy comes in these forms . . .

<u>Some students might know that some forms of energy are heat, light, sound, electrical,</u>
<u>mechanical, solar, and chemical.</u>

_____

_____

_____

Energy changes forms when these things happen . . .

<u>Answers will vary. Students might mention turning on a light, burning firewood, eating</u>
<u>food, running, using a car, or playing a musical instrument.</u>

_____

_____

_____

Name_____ Date_____

ENERGY TO BURN

Procedure

Record your observations of the wooden match.

Students should describe the characteristics of the match, such as the color of the tip and the color of the wood.

_____

_____

_____

Record your observations of the wooden match as it burns.

Students should describe how the match looks as it burns and how the appearance of the match is changing.

_____

_____

_____

Analyze and Conclude

Write the answers to the questions in your book on the lines below.

1. Students may know that heat generated by striking the match (friction) started the match burning.

_____

_____

2. Accept all reasonable ideas that students can justify.

_____

_____

Name_____ Date_____

FEEL THE BEAT

Procedure

Record your observations of what you feel when you touch the drum after beating it.

Students should feel the top of the drum vibrate.

_____

_____

Write your prediction about what will happen to the confetti after you beat the drum once. Explain your prediction.

Students should explain that they predict the confetti will bounce up and down because the top of the drum bounces up and down when they beat it.

_____

_____

Record your observations of the confetti on top of the drum after you beat the drum once.

Students should observe the confetti bounce up and down.

_____

_____

Analyze and Conclude

Write the answers to the questions in your book on the lines below.

1. Students were feeling the vibrations of the drum. The energy to start the drum vibrating comes from hitting it with the stick.

_____

_____

ACTIVITY RECORD

Name_____ Date_____

2. The confetti bounced around. Students may have predicted this movement. They may have predicted that the confetti would move around more or less than it did.

_____

_____

_____

3. The confetti was moved by vibrations.

_____

_____

Name_____ Date_____

MYSTERY CAN

Procedure

Write your prediction about what will happen if you roll the can away from you across the floor. Explain your prediction.

Some students might predict that the can will roll away from them, stop, then roll back toward them because as the can rolls away, the rubber band becomes twisted. Most students will say the can will simply roll away from them.

_____

_____

_____

Record your observations as you roll the can on the floor.

Students should observe the can roll away from them, stop, then roll back toward them.

_____

_____

_____

Analyze and Conclude

Write the answers to the questions in your book on the lines below.

1. Students should find that the can rolled away from them, stopped, and then rolled back toward them. They may or may not have predicted this behavior.

_____

_____

_____

_____

ACTIVITY RECORD

Name_____ Date_____

2. Students might infer that the metal washers are causing the rubber band to twist as the can rolls, and as the rubber band untwists, the can rolls back.

_____

_____

3. Students should recognize that their push was the energy that started the can moving. They might conclude that the can rolled back because the rubber band untwisted.

_____

_____

INVESTIGATE FURTHER!

RESEARCH

Page C9

List all the toys you can think of that move. Next to each toy, **describe** what you think causes it to move.

Toy	Cause of Motion
Answers may include:	Answers may include:
ball	person throwing it
roller skates	person moving them
remote control car	batteries
wind-up toy	wound up a spring
bicycle	person pedaling it
TV videogame	electricity and person controlling the game

Infer what energy has to do with each toy you listed.

Students should infer that energy is required to move all of the toys they listed.

Name_____ Date_____

INVESTIGATION 1
·····························

1. Use an example to explain how stored energy can change to energy of motion.

Examples may be similar to the following. A child standing at the top of a hill with a sled has stored energy. As the child pushes off and sleds down the hill, the stored energy is converted to energy of motion.

_____

_____

2. Think about all the things you do from the time you get up in the morning until you arrive at school. Write a short story about your activities and identify all the forms of energy you use.

Students might mention using heat and electrical energy when using a hair dryer; electrical and sound energy when watching the weather forecast on television; mechanical and chemical energy when riding in a school bus or car; and light and electrical energy when using lights.

_____

_____

_____

Make a word web showing the relationships among the words *energy, energy of motion, stored energy, heat energy, sound energy, light energy, electrical energy, mechanical energy,* and *chemical energy*.

Students should show that energy of motion and stored energy are two types of energy. Heat energy, sound energy, light energy, electrical energy, and mechanical energy are all kinds of energy of motion. Chemical energy is stored energy.

© Silver Burdett Ginn

ACTIVITY RECORD

Name_____ Date_____

SAND SHAKE
· ·

Procedure

In the chart below, **record the temperature** of the sand before
you shake it.

Temperature (°C) of Sand	
Before shaking	_____
After shaking Prediction	temperature will increase 1°–2°C higher
Actual	_____

Write your prediction in the chart for what the temperature of
the sand will be if you shake the jar 200 times.

Record the temperature of the sand in the jar after shaking it
200 times.

Analyze and Conclude

Write the answers to the questions in your book on the lines below.

1. Most students will note that the temperature of the sand increased only slightly
(1°–2°C) after being shaken vigorously. If students predicted otherwise, ask them to
explain their reasoning. Students should identify how predictions differ from group to
group.

_____

_____

Name_____ Date_____

2. A few students may hypothesize that the sand got warmer because all the grains were
being moved around very fast, and that the energy of motion changed to heat energy.
Most students should recognize that heat is caused by friction as the sand grains rub
against each other.

_____

_____

_____

Name_____ Date_____

UNIT PROJECT LINK
....

List all the kinds of energy that will be used in your model home.

<u>Students will probably list electrical, mechanical, light, heat, and chemical.</u>

_____

_____

Think of what can happen to the energy used in your home. How might this energy be wasted?

<u>Answers will vary. Possible answers include leaving on lights and appliances when gone, keeping the house too warm in winter or too cool in summer, and losing warm air through leaky doors and windows.</u>

_____

_____

_____

List your ideas for how a home can be built to save energy.

<u>Answers will vary. Students might suggest using insulation and energy-saving windows among other things.</u>

_____

_____

_____

_____

_____

Share this information with your group.

Name_____ Date_____

SUN POWER

Procedure

Record the temperature of the sand before you place it in sunlight.

Students should record the temperature in °C.

Write your prediction for how the temperature of the sand will change after being in sunlight for ten minutes.

Some students might predict that the temperature of the sand will increase.

Record the temperature of the sand after if has been in sunlight for ten minutes.

The temperature of the sand should increase.

Make a drawing to show why the temperature of the sand changed.

Students' drawings should indicate that energy from sunlight caused the temperature of the sand to increase.

ACTIVITY RECORD

Name_____ Date_____

Analyze and Conclude

Write the answers to the questions in your book on the lines below.

1. The temperature of the sand increased.
_____

_____

2. Some of the Sun's energy (infrared) was absorbed by the sand and converted to heat energy. Students should connect this same process to their feeling warm when sitting in the Sun.
_____

_____

_____

Name_____ Date_____

THINK IT WRITE IT

INVESTIGATION 2
• •

1. Explain the energy changes that occur when you turn on a fan.

The switch starts electrical energy flowing into the fan's motor, which responds by
turning (mechanical energy), and, in the process, the fan's motor gives off heat.

_____

_____

2. Think about the many ways that energy can change form at home or at school. Make a list of these changes. What form of energy is involved most often?

Students' answers might include the following examples of energy changes: chemical
energy changes to heat energy when gas, coal, or wood is burned; electrical energy
changes to mechanical energy when people use some appliances, such as a fan or
refrigerator; electrical energy changes to heat energy when people use appliances such
as a stove, or a clothes dryer; light energy changes to chemical energy when plants
make food; and electrical energy changes to light energy when a light bulb is turned
on. Heat energy is involved in almost every energy change.

_____

_____

_____

Use a flow chart to show the energy changes that occur when
people use solar energy to heat their homes.

Solar energy ⟶ light energy ⟶ heat energy

© Silver Burdett Ginn

CHAPTER WRAP-UP

Name_____ Date_____

ENERGY
••••••••••••••••••

What is energy?

Energy is the ability to move something or cause a change in matter. Energy of motion is the energy that moving matter has. Stored energy is the energy in matter that can cause that matter to move or change.

_____

_____

What are the different forms of energy?

Light, sound, heat, chemical, mechanical, electrical, and solar

_____

_____

_____

What can happen to energy?

Energy can change from one form to another. When energy changes form, no energy is ever lost, or used up.

_____

_____

Look at the picture you drew on page 107. What forms of energy are the objects using?

Answers will vary depending on what students have drawn. Most students will have drawn amusement park rides which use electricity to make mechanical energy.

_____

_____

Name_____ Date_____

Think about what you learned in Chapter 1 when you answer the following questions.

1. What did you learn about energy that interested you the most? Explain why it was interesting.

Answers will vary. Students should explain what topic about energy interested them
the most.

_____

_____

_____

_____

2. Describe the ideas about energy that were difficult to understand. Tell how you could help yourself understand these ideas better.

Answers will vary. Students might suggest reading more about the topic they have
difficulties with, or they might do more experimenting, or ask questions of an expert.

_____

_____

_____

_____

3. What else would you like to learn about the forms of energy and how energy changes form? What could you do to find out?

Answers will vary. Some students might suggest reading additional sources, doing some
other experimenting, or speaking to an engineer or physicist.

_____

_____

_____

_____

Name_____ Date_____

HEAT AND TEMPERATURE

Imagine that you can see heat. Draw how heat moves in this picture.

Students' drawings should show warmed particles of air moving out of the fireplace and rising. As the particles cool, they sink back toward the floor.

Name_____ Date_____

Dear Journal,

I think that heat is . . .

Some students might know that heat is a form of energy that causes particles of matter to
move faster.

_____

_____

_____

Heat moves in these ways . . .

Some students might describe conduction (the movement of heat by direct contact
between particles of matter), convection (the movement of heat through liquids and gases
by the movements of particles), or radiation (the movement of heat in the form of waves).

_____

_____

_____

I can keep warm in these ways . . .

Students might describe dressing in layers; wearing heavy, thick clothing; sitting in a
sunny spot; drinking or eating something warm; or wrapping up in a blanket.

_____

_____

_____

Heat changes matter in these ways . . .

Students might suggest that heat melts solids, evaporates liquids, helps mix different
kinds of matter together, and changes matter into different kinds of matter.

_____

_____

_____

Name_____ Date_____

BOTTLE THERMOMETER

Procedure

Write your predictions about what will happen to the water level in the straw if you put your bottle thermometer in ice water, then in warm water.

Some students might predict that the water level in the straw will drop when the thermometer is in ice water, and it will rise when the bottle thermometer is in warm water.

_____

_____

Record your observations when you place the bottle thermometer in ice water.

The water level in the straw drops.

_____

_____

Record your observations when you place the bottle thermometer in warm water.

The water level in the straw rises.

_____

_____

Analyze and Conclude

Write the answers to the questions in your book on the lines below.

1. When the bottle was cooled, the water level in the bottle thermometer went down. When the bottle was warmed, the water level rose.

_____

_____

_____

Name_____ Date_____

2. The water took up less space when the bottle thermometer was cooled, as shown by the drop in the water level. When the bottle was warmed, the water took up more space, as shown by the rise in the water level.

_____

_____

3. Students might hypothesize that the heat caused the water level to rise, just as the liquid in a real thermometer does. They should also mention that the water dropped when the bottle thermometer was placed in a cold place, just as the liquid in a real thermometer does.

_____

_____

INVESTIGATE FURTHER!
. . . .
EXPERIMENT
Page C25

Predict what will happen if you place the bottle thermometer in sunlight.
Students should predict that the water level in the straw will rise.

Record your observations of the water level in the straw when you place the bottle thermometer in sunlight.
The water level in the straw rises.

Infer what caused the water level in the straw to change.
Students should infer that sunlight warmed the water in the bottle thermometer, causing the water to take up more space.

Name_____ Date_____

A HOT TOPIC
....

Procedure

Write your predictions about what will happen to the temperature of a washer and a pencil eraser after you rub them on a piece of paper. Explain your predictions.

Students might predict that the eraser will feel hot, and the washer slightly warm after
rubbing them on a piece of paper.

_____

_____

_____

_____

Record how the washer feels before and after you rub it on paper.

Before   The washer should feel cool.

_____

After   The washer should feel slightly warm.

_____

Record how the eraser feels before and after you rub it on paper.

Before   The eraser should feel like room temperature.

_____

After   The eraser should feel hot.

_____

Name_____ Date_____

Analyze and Conclude

Write the answers to the questions in the book on the lines below.

1. The washer felt cool at first, then slightly warmer after rubbing. The eraser felt like room temperature before, but quite hot after rubbing.

_____

_____

_____

2. The eraser felt warmer than the washer after rubbing because the eraser has a rougher surface.

_____

_____

_____

INVESTIGATION CLOSE

Name_____ Date_____

INVESTIGATION 1
....

1. What are two ways to make matter warm? Explain what happens to particles of matter when they are warmed.

<u>Using microwaves or friction; when warmed, particles of matter move faster and move</u>
farther apart than when matter is cool.

_____

_____

2. Draw pictures to show what happens to the particles of water in a bottle thermometer when heat is added and when it's taken away.

Drawings should show that particles move farther apart and faster when heat is added
and closer together and slower when heat is removed.

Draw diagrams to show the particles in a solid, a liquid, and a gas.

Students should draw the solid with particles that are very close together, the liquid with
particles farther apart, and the gas with particles farthest apart.

ACTIVITY RECORD

Name_____ Date_____

HEAT TAKES A TRIP

Procedure

In the chart below, **write your prediction** about how the dry
ends of the metal spoon, the wooden stick, and the plastic spoon
will feel after placing them in hot water.

Object	Prediction	Observation
Metal spoon	might predict warm	should feel warm
Wooden stick	might predict cool	should feel cool
Plastic spoon	might predict cool	should feel cool

Record your observations in the chart of how the dry ends of
the metal spoon, the wooden stick, and the plastic spoon feel
after placing them in hot water.

Analyze and Conclude

Write the answers to the questions in your book on the lines below.

1. After five minutes in hot water the metal spoon felt the warmest and the plastic felt
the coolest.

_____

_____

ACTIVITY RECORD

Name_____ Date_____

2. Some students might be surprised at how warm the metal spoon felt.

_____

_____

_____

3. Students should infer that pans are made of metal because heat moves better through metal to cook food, but handles are made of wood or plastic to stay cooler to the touch.

_____

_____

Name_____ Date_____

SIDE BY SIDE

Procedure

Based on the model, **draw a diagram** to show how heat moves through a solid.

Students should draw a heat source near a solid material. Particles within the solid near the heat source should receive heat energy and pass it to adjacent particles until all the particles in the solid have received heat energy.

Analyze and Conclude

Write the answer to the question in your book on the lines below.

A pan warms up as heat moves from the burner to the metal pan.

_____

_____

CHAPTER 2

Name _____ Date _____

WET OR DRY

Procedure

Record the temperature readings of thermometer *A* and thermometer *B*.

Thermometer *A*   <u>Both thermometers should show the same temperature.</u>

Thermometer *B*   _____

Record the temperature readings of thermometer *A* and thermometer *B* after laying a wet cloth on *A* and a dry cloth on *B*.

Thermometer *A* with wet cloth   <u>should have lower temperature</u>

Thermometer *B* with dry cloth   <u>should have higher temperature</u>

Analyze and Conclude

Write the answers to the questions in your book on the lines below.

1. <u>Water particles that evaporated from wet cloth took in surrounding heat. Remaining</u> water particles had less energy, so the temperature under the cloth dropped.

_____

_____

2. <u>Water molecules evaporating from the wet swimsuit take in energy (heat) from your</u> body, making you feel cool.

_____

_____

Name_____ Date_____

A SWEET ACTIVITY!

Procedure

Write your prediction for how many spoonfuls of sugar will dissolve in the cold water.

Students will predict any number of spoonfuls of sugar.

Record the number of spoonfuls of sugar you add to cold water until no more will dissolve.

Students shouldn't count the spoonful of sugar that doesn't completely dissolve.

Write your prediction for how many spoonfuls of sugar will dissolve in the warm water.

Students should predict that more spoonfuls of sugar will dissolve in the warm water.

Record the number of spoonfuls of sugar that dissolve in the warm water.

More spoonfuls of sugar should dissolve in the warm water than in the cold water.

Make a drawing to show your results of adding sugar to cold water and to warm water.

Students' drawings should show that the particles of water are farther apart in warm water than in cold water, so there is more room for sugar particles in warm water.

Name_____ Date_____

Analyze and Conclude

Write the answers to the questions in your book on the lines below.

1. The warm water dissolved more sugar. Comparison of results with predictions depends on what students predicted.

_____

_____

2. More sugar dissolves in warmer water because the particles in warm water are farther apart than those in cold water, making more space for the sugar.

_____

_____

Name_____ Date_____

INVESTIGATION 3

1. List and describe five different ways that matter can change when heat is added or subtracted.

Ice can melt, liquid water can evaporate, or wood can change into ashes when heat is added. Liquid water can freeze, or water vapor can condense when heat is subtracted.

_____

_____

_____

_____

2. Infer and explain why sidewalks are made with spaces between the sections of concrete.

In the summer when the sidewalks get hot, the concrete expands. The spaces between the sections give the concrete room to expand without breaking.

_____

_____

Make a drawing to show how water changes from a liquid to a gas.

Students' drawings should show particles of water moving fast enough to escape from the liquid into the air.

Name_____ Date_____

HEAT AND TEMPERATURE
••

What is heat?

Heat is the amount of energy in the particles making up matter. The particles in a gas have more heat energy that the particles in a solid because the gas particles move faster than the particles in a solid.

How can heat be produced?

Heat can be produced by friction, a force that works against the movement of two objects when the objects touch.

How can heat move?

Heat moves by conduction (the movement of heat by direct contact between particles of matter), convection (the movement of heat through liquids and gases by the movements of particles), and radiation (the movement of heat in the form of waves).

How can heat change materials?

When heat energy is added to matter it can melt solids, evaporate liquids, expand matter, change matter completely, or help matter mix together. When heat energy is taken away from matter it can freeze liquids, condense gases, and contract matter.

Name_____ Date_____

Think about what you learned in Chapter 2 when you answer the following questions.

1. Describe what part of this chapter about heat and temperature you liked best.

Answers will vary. Some students might describe a certain activity that they liked best.

_____

_____

2. What was the most useful thing you learned about heat and temperature? Explain.

Answers will vary. Some students might describe how heat moves or how heat changes materials.

_____

_____

3. Tell what ideas about heat and temperature were hard to understand. How could you better understand these ideas?

Answers will vary. Students might suggest rereading parts of the chapter, redoing activities, reading additional sources, or asking questions.

_____

_____

_____

4. What else would you like to know about heat and tempera-ture? How could you find out about this?

Answers will vary. Students might suggest reading additional sources, doing more experimenting, or talking with an engineer or a heating and air conditioning specialist.

_____

_____

CHAPTER PREVIEW

Name_____ Date_____

USING AND SAVING ENERGY

Imagine that you live in the 22nd Century and gasoline is scarce. Draw the most common form of transportation in this century.

Students' drawings will vary. They should illustrate some kind of vehicle that is powered by an alternative energy source.

Name_____ Date_____

Dear Journal,

I think fossil fuels are . . .

Some students might know that oil, coal, and natural gas are fossil fuels.

_____

_____

Besides fossil fuels, people get energy from these sources . . .

Students might list solar energy, wind energy, water energy, nuclear energy, and geothermal energy.

_____

_____

Most of the energy I use comes from these energy sources . . .

Some students will know that they use fossil fuels for most of their energy needs.

_____

_____

_____

I can save energy by doing these things . . .

Possible answers include turning off lights when leaving a room, car pooling, taking a bus or a train, taking short showers, closing the refrigerator door quickly, and taking the stairs instead of an elevator.

_____

_____

_____

ACTIVITY RECORD

Name_____ Date_____

ENERGY COUNT

Procedure

In the chart below, **record** all the ways you've used energy today.

Ways I've Used Energy Today	Where the Energy Comes From
Answers may include the following	
walking	food
riding in a car	gasoline
listening to a tape recorder	batteries or electricity
turning on lights	electricity
alarm clock	batteries or electricity

Record in the chart where you think the energy comes from for the activities you listed in the first column.

Analyze and Conclude

Write the answers to the questions in your book on the lines below.

1. Students should recognize that they get energy from the food they eat, that most appliances are powered by electricity, that toys often use batteries, and that motor vehicles use gasoline as an energy source.

2. They could walk or ride a bicycle instead of using motor vehicles, or they could use a mechanical pencil sharpener rather than an electric one.

Name_____ Date _____

INVESTIGATION 1

1. List different energy sources people use. Which one do you think is best? Explain.

Energy sources include solar energy, wind energy, hydroelectric energy, nuclear energy, geothermal energy, and the fossil fuels oil, coal, and natural gas. Accept all "best" choices that students can justify.

2. Pretend the people in your town or city use oil to heat their homes. You are told that fossil fuels have run out as an energy source. Make a plan for your town to get energy in another way. Explain how it could be done.

Students' plans should include the use of alternative energy sources, such as solar energy, wind energy, nuclear energy, and hydroelectric energy. Plans will depend on students' geographic locations and proximity to alternative energy sources. Accept all reasonable plans.

Make a chart to classify different kinds of energy sources as either fossil fuels or alternative fuels.

Students should show that fossil fuels and alternative fuels are two kinds of energy sources. Fossil fuels include coal, oil, and natural gas. Alternative energy sources include solar energy, wind energy, nuclear energy, geothermal energy, and water energy.

ACTIVITY RECORD

CHAPTER 3

Name_____ Date_____

SAVING FUEL

Procedure

In the space below, **calculate** which way to get to the zoo—by car, van or bus—will use the least amount of fuel.

Students should calculate that to get to the zoo, it will take 10 cars using 4 gallons of fuel each for a total of 40 gallons of fuel one way and 80 gallons round trip; 5 vans using 5 gallons of fuel each for a total of 25 gallons of fuel one way and 50 gallons round trip; and 1 bus using a total of 10 gallons one way and 20 gallons round trip.

Record your choice for the way to get to the zoo that uses the least amount of fuel.

The bus would use the least amount of fuel.

Analyze and Conclude

Write the answers to the questions in your book on the lines below.

1. The bus would use the least amount of fuel.

2. The more people that ride a bus, the more fuel efficient it becomes. Public transportation such as buses might not be available in their communities or may not be available at all times.

Name_____ Date_____

KEEP IT COOL

Procedure

Write your plan for keeping an ice cube from melting.

Students might choose to wrap the ice cube in one or a combination of the insulating
materials.

_____

_____

_____

Record the width of the ice cube before you start your plan.

Students should record the width of the ice cube in centimeters.

Record the width of the ice cube 10 minutes after using your
plan to keep the ice cube from melting.

Students should observe that the ice cube is somewhat smaller than before.

Analyze and Conclude

Write the answers to the questions in your book on the lines below.

1. Groups' results will vary. Most likely the plastic foam would be the best insulator followed
by the cotton balls, cloth, and paper towels.

_____

_____

2. Students should hypothesize that similar materials will work in the walls of a house to
reduce the rate at which heat energy is transferred.

_____

_____

UNIT PROJECT LINK

Name_____ Date_____

UNIT PROJECT LINK
....

List below as many ways as you can think of to save energy
in the home.

Answers will vary. Possible answers include turning off lights when leaving a room,
taking short showers, turning the thermostat down at night, adding insulation to the
walls, and keeping drafts from entering through windows and doors.

_____

_____

_____

_____

_____

_____

What could you do in your model home to use some of your
energy-saving ideas?

Answers will vary. Possible answers include adding insulation to windows, walls, and
doors; and filling cracks in the house with caulk.

_____

_____

_____

_____

_____

Share this information with your group.

Name_____ Date_____

INVESTIGATION 2

1. Explain why coal, oil, and natural gas are called fossil fuels.

A fossil is the remains of a plant or animal that lived many years ago. Fossil fuels form from long-dead plant and animal remains.

_____

_____

2. Give at least two reasons why saving energy is wise. Make a list of ways you plan to save energy.

Saving energy can help conserve resources, save money, and reduce pollution. Accept all reasonable answers.

_____

_____

_____

_____

_____

Draw a diagram to show how coal is formed.

Students' diagrams might look something like this.

Remains of once-living ⟶ covered with layers ⟶ extreme pressure ⟶ coal
swamp plants   of mud and sand   and heat

CHAPTER WRAP-UP

Name_____ Date_____

USING AND SAVING ENERGY
••

What energy sources do people use?

People use fossil fuels (coal, oil, and natural gas), wind energy, solar energy, water energy, nuclear energy, and geothermal energy.

_____

_____

What are fossil fuels?

Fossil fuels are fuels that formed from decayed plants and animals that lived long ago. Oil, coal, and natural gas are three types of fossil fuels.

_____

_____

How can people save energy?

Some ways people can save energy include insulating their houses, turning down the temperature setting for the furnace in winter, using fluorescent light bulbs, turning out lights, checking windows and doors for leaks, quickly closing the refrigerator door, car-pooling, using public transportation, driving the speed limit, and walking instead of riding in a car.

_____

_____

_____

_____

_____

_____

_____

CHAPTER WRAP-UP

Name_____ Date_____

Think about what you learned in Chapter 3 when you answer the following questions.

1. What did you learn about saving energy that you will be able to use in your own life?

Answers will vary. Students should describe one or two ways that they can help save energy.

_____

_____

_____

_____

2. Tell what surprised you the most as you read about using and saving energy.

Answers will vary. Some students might be surprised about the kinds of alternative energy sources, the length of time required to form fossil fuels, or how soon we could run out of fossil fuels.

_____

_____

3. Describe what else you would like to know about energy sources or how to save energy. How would you find out about this?

Answers will vary. Some students might suggest reading additional sources or speaking to an engineer or someone from the electric company.

_____

_____

_____

_____

_____

Name_____ Date_____

UNIT PROJECT WRAP-UP

Think about the model house you helped design and build.
What part of the project did you like best? Explain.

Answers will vary. Some students might like designing the house best, others might like building it best.

_____

_____

Which model house was the most energy-efficient? How do
you know?

Students should explain that the house in which the ice cube took the longest time to melt is the most energy-efficient.

_____

_____

Describe how the most energy-efficient house was built to
save energy.

Students should describe the energy-saving ideas used to design the house.

_____

_____

How would you change your model house to make it even
more energy-efficient?

Answers will vary. Students should describe ways in which they can improve the energy-efficiency of their model house.

_____

_____

Name_____ Date_____

EARTH'S WATER

In Unit D you'll learn about Earth's water resources and how they must be cared for. For the Unit Project Big Event, you'll design a water system for the imaginary town of Waterville. Why do you think a well planned water system is important to a town?

Answers may vary. Students might suggest that people need safe drinking water and
water for household and garden needs; many businesses need water to carry out
their tasks; water is needed by fire departments and parks.

_____

_____

Where are some places that towns get water?

Some students may know that most towns get water from lakes, rivers, reservoirs, or
underground aquifers.

_____

How can people help to save water?

People can help by using water wisely. For example, they can take quick showers
instead of baths, install water-saving faucets and toilets, and plant gardens that do
not require a lot of watering.

_____

How can people help protect water from pollution?

Students might suggest that people can protect water from pollution by taking
dangerous chemicals to a hazardous waste collection site or by reducing their use of
harmful chemicals.

_____

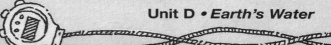

Name_____ Date_____

UNIT PREVIEW
....

There are probably many things you already know about
water. What are some other things you would like to learn?
List your ideas on the lines below.

_____

_____

_____

_____

_____

_____

_____

_____

_____

_____

Name_____ Date_____

WATER, WATER, EVERYWHERE

Find all the things that contain water in this picture and color them blue.

Students should color the steam from the tea kettle, ice cubes, water from the faucet, fruits and vegetables and other food items, father and daughter, pet and water dish, and plant. Some students might even color the entire picture since air contains water vapor.

Name_____ Date_____

Dear Journal,

I think Earth is called the water planet because . . .

Some students might know that Earth is the only planet in our solar system known to have
liquid water; nearly three-fourths of Earth is covered with water.

_____

_____

Most of Earth's water is . . .

Answers may vary. Many students will state that most of Earth's water is found in oceans
and contains salt, which makes it unfit for direct human use.

_____

_____

_____

The three states, or forms of water are . . .

Most students may know that water is found as a liquid, a solid, (ice), and a gas (water
vapor).

_____

_____

I think the water cycle is . . .

Some students may know that the water cycle is the never-ending path that water follows
as it evaporates into the air, condenses into clouds, and returns to Earth as rain.

_____

_____

_____

_____

Name_____ Date_____

THE WATER PLANET

Procedure

Record your estimate of what part of Earth's surface is covered with water.

Some students might know that about three-fourths of Earth's surface is covered with water.

Make a drawing to record how you laid the cutouts of land and water on the table to compare the amount of water to the amount of land.

Students' drawings will vary depending on the methods they used to compare the cutouts of land and water. Their drawings should indicate that about one-fourth of Earth is covered by land and about three-fourths is covered by water.

Analyze and Conclude

Write the answers to the questions in your book on the lines below.

1. Most of the pie graphs should show three-fourths of Earth covered by water.

2. The estimates should compare well because students based them on a world map. The cutouts helped students check their estimates.

3. Students may infer that Earth is called the water planet because most of it is covered with water.

Record your estimate of what fraction of your state is covered by water.

Students' estimates will vary, but in general, most states have more land than water.

Draw a pie graph to show your estimate.

Students' graphs should reflect their estimates.

Check your estimate in the same way as you did in the activity The Water Planet. **Describe** how your estimate compares with what you find.

Students should explain how accurate their estimates were.

Name_____ Date_____

DRY UP!
. . . .

Procedure

Record the mass of the carrot slice.

Students should record the carrot slice mass in grams.

Record the mass of the carrot slice after it has been in a sunny, dry place for two days.

The mass of the carrot slice should be less than the first time students measured it.

Analyze and Conclude

Write the answers to the questions in your book on the lines below.

1. The change in mass is due to the loss of water.

2. Students may infer that since carrots are largely water, it is likely that water makes up part of other plants. They may also reason that because plants must be watered to survive, it is likely that other plants contain water.

3. Since plants are living things, students might infer that animals, including humans, also contain water. Students may also infer that since they drink water, human beings must contain water.

Name_____ Date_____

INVESTIGATION 1

1. Earth is called the water planet, yet finding enough drinking water for everyone on the planet is sometimes a problem. Explain why.

Even though three-fourths of Earth is covered by water, most of the water is salt water. Most of the world's fresh water is frozen in ice caps and glaciers. Therefore, drinking water can be scarce in certain places.

2. Pretend you are a water-use detective. List four ways that people use water. Why is water so important?

People use water for drinking, personal cleanliness, cooking and cleaning, growing plants, producing power, cooling machines, mining, manufacturing, and so on. Water is important because it is necessary for people to survive and for its other uses.

Draw a pie graph to show how water is used in your home.

Students' graphs will vary, but in general, the greatest amounts of water used in the home are for showers and baths, laundry, toilets, and outdoor watering. Students should also include dish washing, drinking, cooking, and cleaning.

CHAPTER 1

Name_____ Date_____

DISAPPEARING ACT
. . . .

Procedure

Write your prediction about in which cup—the one in the warm place or the one in the cool place—the water level will change the most.

Most students will probably predict that the water level will change most in the cup in the warm place.

_____

_____

Record your observations of the water level in each cup after two days.

Students should observe that the water level in the cup in the warm place is lower than the water level in the cup in the cool place.

_____

_____

Analyze and Conclude

Write the answers to the questions in your book on the lines below.

1. Both cups had lower water levels, but the water level was lowest in the cup placed in the warmer area.

_____

_____

2. A warmer temperature causes more water to disappear than a cooler temperature does.

_____

_____

Name_____ Date_____

WATER UPS AND DOWNS

Procedure

Make a drawing of your setup, showing the plastic jar, the aluminum foil cover, the hot water, and the ice cubes.

Students' drawings should show the plastic jar with hot water in it and covered by a molded piece of aluminum foil holding a few ice cubes.

Record your observations of what happens on the underside of the aluminum foil cover when you place some ice cubes in it.

Students should observe drops of water condensing on the underside of the foil.

_____

Analyze and Conclude

Write the answers to the questions in your book on the lines below.

1. Students should hypothesize that water gets into the air through evaporation.

_____

2. Students may infer that evaporation occurs faster during the day because of the Sun's heat. This inference should be based on the warm water in the jar, which represents a lake or ocean warmed by the Sun.

_____

INVESTIGATION 2

Name_____ Date_____

1. If water runs downhill to the oceans, why don't oceans overflow?

The processes of evaporation and condensation which occur during the water cycle keep the ocean from overflowing.

_____

_____

2. Draw a picture of the water cycle. Then explain the changes a drop of water goes through as it moves through the cycle.

Students' drawings should include the following ideas: Energy from the Sun makes some of the water in a body of water evaporate as water vapor. Some of the water vapor condenses to form a cloud. In time water droplets in the cloud get larger, then fall to Earth as precipitation. Then the cycle repeats.

Describe water in each of the three basic states in which matter exists.

Students should describe liquid water as having no definite shape, but a definite volume; solid water, or ice, as having both a definite shape and volume; and gaseous water, or water vapor, as having neither a definite shape nor volume.

_____

_____

Name_____ Date_____

WELL, WELL

Procedure

Write your prediction of what will happen when you add water to the sand around your model well.

Answers may vary. Students might predict that water will come into their well.

_____

Record your observations of what you see when you look into your well.

Students should see water in their wells.

_____

Make a drawing of your model well to show how the water moved into it.

Students should show a cross section of the cup pushed into the sand and draw lines or arrows to show how the water moved down through the sand and entered the cup. The water level in the sand should be level with the water level in the cup.

Analyze and Conclude

Write the answers to the questions in your book on the lines below.

1. Students will see water in their well at the same level as the surface of the sand.

_____

ACTIVITY RECORD

Name_____ Date_____

2. Students should infer that the water came from the surrounding sand.

_____

3. Students may respond that rain keeps the well supplied with water.

_____

4. Students may predict that if it doesn't "rain" for a few days there will be little or no
water in the well, because rain supplies the water that trickles through the sand.

_____

_____

INVESTIGATE FURTHER!
....
EXPERIMENT

Page D21

Tell what kind of soil you used for your model
well this time.

Students will identify clay soil or topsoil.

Describe what happened after you poured water on the
soil of this model well.

Students should again observe water in the well, though there may not be as much
and it may have taken longer to filter in.

Infer which kind of soil works best with a well. Explain.

Most students will infer that a sandy soil works best because water passes through
this type of soil quickly and not as much of the water is absorbed by the soil.
However, sandy soil will work only if it's saturated and there's an impermeable layer
of rock under it. Otherwise, the water will drain away and the well will be dry.

Name_____ Date_____

SOAK IT UP!

Procedure

In the chart below, **record your measurement** of the water that passed through the funnel half filled with gravel.

Earth Material	Water That Passed Through in One Minute (in mL)
Gravel	Students should find that the most water passed through the gravel and the least through the soil.
Sand	
Soil	

Write your predictions about what will happen if you repeat the activity, first using sand and then using soil.

Most students will predict that less water will pass through the funnel with sand than with gravel and even less with soil.

Record all your measurements in the chart.

Analyze and Conclude

Write the answers to the questions in your book on the lines below.

1. Water should pass most rapidly through gravel and most slowly through soil.

2. The soil held water best because less water passed through it.

3. When rainwater falls, it soaks into and passes through different kinds of ground at different rates. Rainwater passes through sand and gravel more quickly than through soil.

Name_____ Date_____

UNIT PROJECT LINK

What sources of water could a town use for its water system?
List as many different water sources as you can think of.

Students could suggest rivers, lakes, reservoirs, wells (ground water), and desalinated
ocean water as possible water sources.

_____

_____

_____

List some questions your company will need to have
answered before you can select a source of water for
Waterville.

Students' questions may vary. For example they might ask if there are any lakes or
rivers nearby, is there a sufficient supply of ground water, and so on.

_____

_____

_____

_____

_____

_____

_____

_____

_____

Share this information with your group.

Name_____ Date_____

INVESTIGATION 3

1. Describe three different ways in which towns and cities can get water for their people to use.

<u>Towns and cities can get water from desalination plants, from wells, and from nearby</u>
freshwater sources.

_____

_____

2. Imagine you are in charge of finding a water supply for your town. You live in an area that gets lots of rain, but there are no surface-water supplies nearby. Describe and draw a picture of what you would do to get water flowing to your town.

The picture should show a drawing of a well. Water pipes might be shown leading away
from the well.

Look up the word *aqueduct* in a dictionary. Tell how aqueducts are used.

<u>Students should describe how water flows in aqueducts from water sources to cities.</u>

_____

_____

CHAPTER WRAP-UP

Name_____ Date_____

WATER, WATER, EVERYWHERE

Where is water found on Earth?

Earth is about three-fourths covered with water in oceans, lakes, and rivers. There is water underground and frozen in icecaps and glaciers.

_____

_____

_____

Why is water important?

All living things need water to stay alive.

_____

_____

_____

What is the water cycle?

The water cycle is the never-ending path that water follows as it evaporates into the air, condenses into clouds, and returns to Earth as rain.

_____

_____

_____

Where are sources of fresh water found?

Fresh water is found in rivers, lakes, reservoirs, and aquifers. Fresh water can also be obtained by desalinating ocean water.

_____

_____

_____

CHAPTER WRAP-UP

Name_____ Date_____

Think about what you learned in Chapter 1 when you answer the following questions.

1. What did you learn about sources of water on Earth that you didn't know before?

Answers may vary. Some students may not have known that so much of Earth's surface is covered with water and yet so little of it can be used by people.

_____

_____

_____

2. What will you think of now every time you turn on a water faucet?

Answers may vary. Students might think of where the water comes from, such as a lake, reservoir, or aquifer.

_____

_____

3. How will a cloud now remind you of the water cycle?

Students might state that a cloud is a part of the water cycle that forms when water vapor in the air condenses and that water returns to Earth's surface from a cloud in the form of rain.

_____

_____

4. Look again at the picture on page 157. What changes would you make in what you colored?

Answers will vary depending on what students colored previously on the page. Most students will probably want to color additional items that they now know contain water.

_____

_____

Name _____ Date _____

WONDERS OF WATER

How does water get from its source to where it's needed? Draw arrows to trace the flow of water through this town.

WATER TREATMENT PLANT

CAR WASH

Students should indicate the flow of water through pipes from the lake, to the treatment plant, to the water tower, and then to the house, business, and park fountain.

Use with pages D30–D31.

Name_____ Date_____

Dear Journal,

I think the way water gets to my home is . . .

For most students, water travels through pipes from a treatment plant near the source of the water, to a water tower, and then underground to their homes. Some students may get water from wells, and the water travels directly from the wells to their homes.

_____

_____

The way water tastes is due to . . .

The taste of water depends on the chemicals and minerals found in the water. Distilled water, which has no chemicals or minerals in it, is tasteless.

_____

_____

Some things that can cause water to be harmful include . . .

Students might suggest that different microorganisms—or germs—and chemicals and wastes can cause water to be harmful.

_____

_____

I think water is made safe for drinking by . . .

Many students will know that water is filtered to remove harmful substances and treated with chemicals to kill harmful organisms before it is safe for drinking.

_____

_____

ACTIVITY RECORD

Name_____ Date_____

THE PRESSURE'S ON
· ·

Procedure

Write your predictions about what will happen at each hole in the milk carton when the tape is removed.

Students' predictions may vary. Some students might suggest that the water pressure will
be strongest at the bottom hole and weakest at the top hole.

_____

_____

Record your observations of what happens when you remove the tape from all the holes at the same time.

Students should observe that the water streams out farther from the lower holes.

_____

_____

Compare your predictions with your observations.

Answers will vary depending on students' predictions.

_____

_____

_____

Analyze and Conclude

Write the answers to the questions in your book on the lines below.

1. Students should notice that water streams out farther from the lower holes.

_____

_____

Name_____ Date_____

2. Students may hypothesize that the weight of the water increases pressure at the bottom of the carton; water exiting from the lower holes is under greater pressure than the water that exits the upper holes.

3. Students should infer that water pressure would be greatest at the lower floors and least at the upper floors. So, the water flow on the lowest floor would be the strongest.

INVESTIGATE
FURTHER!
· · · · · · · · · · · · · · · · ·
EXPERIMENT

Page D33

Describe your plan for increasing the distance a stream of water can reach.

Students' plans may vary. Some students might suggest having only one hole that is close to the bottom of the carton and filling the carton completely full of water. Others may find out that squeezing the carton makes the water stream come out farther.

Describe your results.

Students' results will vary, depending on their setup.

ACTIVITY RECORD

CHAPTER **2**

Name_____ Date_____

TOWER POWER
. . . .

Procedure

Write your prediction about what will happen when water is poured into the funnel of your model water tower.

Students' predictions may vary. Many will predict that water will stream out of the small
hole in the tape on the end of the tubing.

_____

_____

Record your observations of how the water flows out of the pin-hole as the funnel is lowered and raised.

Students should observe that the water flow is stronger when the funnel is higher and
weaker when the funnel is lower.

_____

_____

Make a drawing of your model water tower to show how height affects the flow of water.

Students' drawings should indicate that the higher the funnel, the stronger the water flow is.

Name _____ Date _____

Analyze and Conclude

Write the answers to the questions in your book on the lines below.

1. <u>Students should note how their predictions compare with their observations.</u>

_____

_____

2. <u>Water flow is increased when the tower is higher.</u>

_____

_____

3. <u>Placing the water storage tower on a building's roof will increase the water flow (water</u> pressure) inside the building.

_____

_____

Name_____ Date_____

UNIT PROJECT LINK

List your ideas about how water is treated so that it's safe
to drink.

Answers may vary. Some students might know that water is treated with chemicals to
disinfect it and remove unwanted substances or that it is filtered.

_____

_____

List your ideas about how water travels from its source to
homes and businesses in a town.

Answers may vary. Students might suggest that water travels underground through a
network of pipes from the point where it is treated to homes and businesses.

_____

_____

How can you find out more about how water is made safe to
drink and delivered to homes and businesses?

Students might suggest contacting a local water department or using library
resources.

_____

List your ideas for how to clean and transport water in
Waterville.

Answers may vary. Students should apply what they know about water treatment and
delivery.

_____

_____

_____

Share this information with your group.

Name_____ Date_____

INVESTIGATION 1

1. Explain how a water tower works to keep water flowing.

A water tower works by using gravity and water pressure to keep water flowing from it.

_____

_____

2. Pretend you work for the water company in your town. People are complaining that they have no water pressure. Describe two different things that could be causing the problem.

Two things that could be causing the problem are leaking pipes and overuse. Both can contribute to a decrease in water pressure.

_____

_____

_____

Make a simple diagram of how you think water gets from its source to your home.

Students' drawings will vary, depending on where their water comes from. Most will show a water treatment plant and underground pipes that lead to their homes. Some may get water from wells, and will show a pipe from the well to their homes.

ACTIVITY RECORD

CHAPTER 2

Name_____ Date_____

WATER TASTE-TEST
....

Procedure

Record your group's ranking of the three water samples you tested.
Use 1 for the water sample you liked best.

1. Students' preferences will vary. Most students will

2. probably rank the distilled water last.

3. _____

Analyze and Conclude

Write the answers to the questions in your book on the lines below.

1. Groups' rankings should reflect taste preferences. Encourage students to discuss what they liked or disliked about the samples so they can see that tastes vary.

2. Bottled spring water may be the preference of most students, though the water fountain sample may also be a popular choice.

3. Students should infer that the samples came from different sources because each tasted different. They might also realize that water can contain invisible (to the eye) ingredients that can affect its taste.

4. Students may be surprised to learn that distilled water they consider "pure" doesn't taste very good. They may also be surprised if they preferred water fountain water over an expensive store-bought spring water.

Name_____ Date_____

HARD AND SOFT WATER

Procedure

Write your prediction for which vial of water—the hard water or the soft water—will have the most suds after being shaken.

<u>Predictions may vary. Students might predict that the soft water will have the most suds.</u>

_____

_____

Record your observations after shaking both vials back and forth the same number of times.

<u>Students should observe that the vial with soft water has the most suds.</u>

_____

_____

Compare your observations with those of other groups.

<u>Students should find their observations consistent with those of other groups.</u>

_____

_____

Analyze and Conclude

Write the answers to the questions in your book on the lines below.

1. <u>Soft water produces more suds than hard water.</u>

_____

_____

ACTIVITY RECORD

Name_____ Date_____

2. Soft water makes washing more efficient._____

_____

_____

3. Bring water samples in clean containers. Use hard and soft water as controls._____

_____

_____

Name_____ Date_____

INVESTIGATION 2
······························

1. A cousin visits you from another town. She says your water tastes different from hers. Explain to her why this may be so.

Students should explain that minerals and chemicals added to water affect its taste. From one town to another, these chemicals and minerals may be different.

_____

_____

2. Water that has no minerals and chemicals tastes as bad as water that has too many minerals and chemicals. Explain what this means.

Water with no minerals or chemicals can taste flat. Water with too many minerals or chemicals can taste unpleasant.

_____

_____

_____

Write a paragraph telling about the best water you ever tasted and the worst water you ever tasted. Where were you when you tasted each of these water samples? How did they each taste?

Students' paragraphs will vary depending on their own personal experiences.

_____

_____

_____

_____

_____

Name_____ Date_____

Let's Clear This Up

Procedure

Write your prediction for what you will see if you pour muddy water through your water-filtering system model.

Predictions may vary. Students might predict that the water will be clearer after it passes
through the filter.

_____

Record your observations of the material that passes through the funnel into the base of the plastic bottle in your model water-filtering system.

Students should observe that the water is clearer than it was before it passed through the
filter.

_____

Analyze and Conclude

Write the answers to the questions in your book on the lines below.

1. Students should compare their predictions to their observations.

_____

2. Students should hypothesize that the materials in the filter prevent some of the
impurities from passing through them.

_____

_____

3. Soil and rocks are filtering materials for the rainwater, just as sand, gravel, and
cheesecloth are the filtering materials in the model.

_____

_____

INVESTIGATE FURTHER

Use with page D47.

Name_____ Date_____

INVESTIGATE FURTHER!

EXPERIMENT

Page D47

List the materials that you use in your filter.

Materials will vary. Students might try cotton gauze pads, cheesecloth, paper towels, coffee filters, newspapers, mesh screening, or other materials.

Record the results of how your filter works.

Results will vary depending on the kinds of materials students use in their filters.

Compare your results with the results of your classmates.

Students should determine how well their filter materials worked in comparison to the materials other students used.

CHAPTER 2

Name_____ Date_____

NOT AS CLEAR AS IT LOOKS
•••

Procedure

Write your predictions for what will happen to the water if you put fertilizer into each cup.

Tap Water: _____Students might predict that the water will not change._____

_____

Aquarium Water: _____Students might predict that the water will turn cloudy._____

_____

Record your observations of the water in each cup after two days.

Tap Water: _____Students should observe that the water is fairly clear._____

_____

Aquarium Water: _____Students should observe that the water is cloudy._____

_____

Analyze and Conclude

Write the answers to the questions in your book on the lines below.

1. _Students should notice that the aquarium water is cloudy and that the tap water is_
clearer.

_____

_____

2. _Living organisms present in aquarium water multiply when fertilizer is added. Tap_
water has been treated in order to remove these organisms.

_____

_____

Name_____ Date_____

INVESTIGATION 3

1. Imagine that you are hiking in the woods. You are very thirsty, and the water in a nearby pond looks very clean. Would you drink it? Why or why not?

<u>You should not drink the water; it may contain harmful bacteria or other organisms</u>

<u>that are too small to see.</u>

_____

_____

2. How are germs in the water killed before the water reaches your home?

<u>Germs are killed by adding chemicals to the water.</u>

_____

_____

In the chart below, describe how each unwanted substance is removed from water to make the water safe to drink.

Water Treatment	
Unwanted substances	Treatment
Twigs, plants, and insects	Filtered out by a screen
Protists and bacteria	Killed by chemicals
Unwanted particles	Mixed with chemicals that cause them to stick together, allowed to settle, and then filtered

Name_____ Date_____

WONDERS OF WATER

How does water move through pipes?

Water is pumped under pressure through pipes to keep it moving or water flows through pipes under pressure due to gravity in a water tower water system. The pipes are buried underground so that the water will not freeze and break the pipes.

_____

_____

How does drinking water vary?

Drinking water can be hard or soft, depending on the amounts of dissolved minerals in the water. Drinking water can also vary in taste, depending on the chemicals and minerals found in the water.

_____

What things in water can be harmful?

Water can contain harmful organisms, such as protists, bacteria, and algae. It can also contain sewage and harmful chemicals.

_____

_____

How is water made safe to drink?

Water is treated with chemicals to disinfect it and cause unwanted particles to stick together and settle to the bottom. Then the water is filtered.

_____

_____

Name_____ Date_____

Think about what you learned in Chapter 2 when you answer the
following questions.

1. What was the most interesting thing you learned about water
as you read this chapter?

Answers will vary. Some students may have found how water gets from its source to
their homes interesting. Others may have liked learning about how water is treated to
make it safe for drinking.

_____

2. What will you think about that you have learned the next
time you drink a glass of water?

Answers will vary. Some students might think about how the water got to them. Others
might consider how the water was made safe to drink.

_____

_____

3. What did you learn that will make you cautious about what
water you drink?

Answers may vary. Many students will discuss the harmful things found in water, such
as protists, bacteria, sewage, and harmful chemicals.

_____

_____

4. What else would you like to learn about water? How can you
find out?

Answers will vary about what students want to learn. They might suggest looking in an
encyclopedia or books on water or talking to an expert to find out more.

_____

_____

_____

Name_____ Date_____

CARING FOR OUR WATER

Students' additions to the drawing may vary. Some possible sources of pollution students might draw include a factory discharging toxic wastes, a sewage pipe, a farmer using harmful chemicals, an open dump, and people dumping litter into the lake.

The water in this lake is polluted. Complete the picture to show some ways in which this water might have become polluted.

Name _____ Date _____

Dear Journal,

I think that acid rain is . . .

Some students might know that acid rain is rainwater or any precipitation that contains pollution, which makes it harmful to many living things and structures.

_____

_____

Some ways that water can become polluted are . . .

Answers may vary. Students might mention industrial, agricultural, and municipal wastes, as well as household and garden chemicals.

_____

_____

Some ways that water pollution spreads from one place to another are . . .

Answers may vary. Some students might know that streams and rivers carry pollution to lakes and oceans. Ocean currents and tides cause pollution to spread through oceans.

_____

_____

Some things that I can do to help reduce water waste and water pollution are . . .

Answers may vary. Students might suggest limiting their use of water when bathing and doing household chores to save water and properly disposing of chemicals and wastes to keep water safe.

_____

_____

_____

_____

ACTIVITY RECORD

CHAPTER **3**

Name_____ Date_____

Not-So-Gentle Rain

Procedure

Write your predictions for what will happen to the seeds in each cup. Explain your predictions.

Tap Water: Predictions may vary. Students might predict the seeds will sprout and grow because tap water is safe for living things.

Acid Rain: Predictions may vary. Students might predict that the seeds will not sprout and grow because acid is harmful to living things.

In the chart below, **record your observations** of the seeds.

Date	Observations	
	Tap Water	Acid Rain
	Students should observe that the seeds sprout and grow normally.	Students should observe that the seeds may sprout but they do not grow normally.

Compare your observations of the seeds to your predictions about them.

Answers will vary depending on students' predictions.

_____

ACTIVITY RECORD

Name_____ Date_____

Analyze and Conclude

Write the answers to the questions in your book on the lines below.

1. Results may vary, but the seeds should grow best in the cup watered with tap water. Students should hypothesize that the vinegar caused the differences in seed growth.

_____

_____

2. Students should infer that acid rain would harm plants by interfering with their growth.

_____

_____

INVESTIGATE FURTHER!
....
RESEARCH

Page D57.

Describe your experiment to find out how much acid rain plants can be watered with and still grow.

Students' experiments may vary, but each should have a control and then vary the amount of acid the other plants receive.

Describe the results of your experiment.

Results will vary, but students should find that the more acid the plants receive, the poorer they will grow.

Name_____ Date_____

INVESTIGATION 1

1. What kinds of water worries could the people of your city or town be having?

People might worry about their water supply becoming polluted or running out.

_____

2. Write a story about what life will be like 100 years from now. Tell whether there will still be water pollution and water worries. What solutions will have been found?

Students' stories should reflect the understanding that unless pollution of water resources is stopped, the pollution problems 100 years from now will be worse.

_____

_____

_____

_____

In nature, acid rain is formed when smoke from factories, homes, and motor vehicles rises into the air. The smoke combines with water drops in the air and in clouds to make acid rain. Then the acid rain falls on living things when it rains. Draw a labeled diagram to show this process.

Students' drawings should illustrate the process described above.

Name_____ Date_____

ALL WASHED UP
....

Procedure

Write your prediction for what effect moving the water containing dirt and oil up onto the "coast" will have on your ocean coastline model.

Predictions may vary. Students might predict that the dirt and oil will coat the coastline materials.

_____

_____

_____

Explain why you made the prediction you did.

Students' explanations may vary. Some might state that the oil and dirt will coat the coastline materials because the oil is sticky.

_____

_____

_____

Record your observations of the coastline materials after you have caused the water to move up onto the coast three or four times.

Students should observe that the coastline materials are coated with oil and dirt.

_____

_____

_____

_____

ACTIVITY RECORD

Name_____ Date_____

Analyze and Conclude

Write the answers to the questions in your book on the lines below.

1. Raising and lowering the pan represented the rise and fall of the tides.

_____

_____

2. The coastline materials have soil and cooking oil on them. Predictions may vary but the materials should be sticky and may be difficult to remove from hands.

_____

_____

_____

3. Tides can carry some forms of pollution up on to the land.

_____

_____

_____

CHAPTER 3

Name_____ Date_____

GOING MY WAY?

Procedure

Write your prediction for what will happen when you take the lid off the jar containing hot, colored water on the bottom of the aquarium.

Predictions may vary. Some students may predict that the hot, colored water from the jar
will rise to the top of the cold water in the aquarium.

_____

_____

_____

Explain why you made the prediction you did.

Explanations may vary. Some students might know that hot water rises in cold water.

_____

_____

_____

Record your observations of what happens when you remove the lid of the jar.

Students should observe that the hot, colored water rises and the cold water sinks.

_____

_____

_____

_____

Name_____ Date_____

Make a drawing of your observations. Add arrows to show how
the water moves.

Students' drawings should show that the hot, colored water rises and the cold water sinks.

Analyze and Conclude

Write the answers to the questions in your book on the lines below.

1. The colored (hot) water rises. The cold water sinks. _____

_____

2. Pollutants could be carried along by these currents or "rivers" of water. _____

_____

_____

Use with page D69.

Name_____ Date_____

UNIT PROJECT LINK

List some ways to protect water from pollution that you could use on Waterville's calendar.

Students' suggestions will vary. Some ways to protect water from pollution include
treating waste water in a sewage-treatment plant, prohibiting factories and businesses
from dumping wastes, reducing agricultural pollution, having safe landfills, and disposing
of hazardous wastes properly.

_____

_____

_____

List some ways to conserve water that you could use on Waterville's calendar.

Students' suggestions may vary. Some ways to conserve water include repairing leaks
and dripping faucets, taking short showers instead of baths, running the dishwasher
and washing machine only with full loads, watering lawns early or late in the day,
and using water-saving devices on showers and in toilets.

_____

_____

_____

List your ideas for how to make Waterville's calendar interesting and attractive.

Students' ideas will vary. They might suggest interesting pictures or funny sayings
for the calendar.

_____

_____

Share this information with your group.

INVESTIGATION CLOSE

INVESTIGATION 2

••••••••••••••••••••••••••••••••••••••

Name_____ Date_____

1. Imagine walking on a beach on the east coast of southern
Florida. You accidentally drop a ball into the ocean. Where
might the ball go?

<u>The ball could go up the eastern coast of the United States. It could even go to Europe.</u>

_____

_____

2. People used to think that the oceans were so big that anything could be dumped into them without harming them.
Explain why this isn't so.

<u>Currents, waves, and tides carry pollution around the world. Scientists have discovered</u>
<u>that the ocean is not able to absorb or break up all the pollutants dumped into it.</u>

_____

_____

_____

Make a drawing to show one way in which water pollution can
spread from one place to another.

Students' drawings may vary, but should illustrate one of the concepts on how water pollution spreads discussed in this investigation.

Name_____ Date_____

DOWN THE DRAIN

Procedure

In the chart below, **record** each activity in which you or others in your home use water during one day. Use the table on page D72 to add to the chart how much water each activity uses.

Water-Using Activity	Number of Times Activity Is Done	Total Water Used for Each Activity
Students should list all water-using activities in their home for one day.	Students should list number of times each activity is done.	Students should record total amount of water used for each activity.

Add up the total amount of water used in your home.

Amounts will vary depending on the number of people in each home and their individual water use.

Analyze and Conclude

Write the answer to the question in your book on the lines below.

Students will probably be surprised by how much water their household uses in one day. Possible answers include taking a bath instead of a shower, or a shorter shower; shutting off the faucet while you brush your teeth; running the washing machine only when you have a full load of clothes.

Name_____ Date_____

DROPS COUNT

Procedure

Write your prediction for how much water is wasted in 30 minutes by a dripping faucet.

Predictions will vary. Students might predict that several gallons of water will be wasted.

_____

Record your measurement of the amount of water in the graduate after one minute.

Measurements will vary depending on the size of the hole in the milk carton.

Analyze and Conclude

Write the answers to the questions in your book on the lines below.

1. Answers may vary but students should record data accurately and do the calculation carefully.

_____

2. A dripping faucet can waste thousands of gallons of water in a year.

_____

_____

Name_____ Date_____

 INVESTIGATION 3
• •

1. Imagine there is a very severe water shortage. You are told
you can use only 2 gal of water each day. Write a story about
how you would live.

Students should describe ways to use water in the most conservative manner.

_____

_____

_____

_____

_____

2. Suppose that you were in charge of saving and protecting
water in your school. What kinds of things might you tell
everybody to do?

Answers could include fixing leaky faucets, putting plastic jugs of water in toilets, not
letting the water run.

_____

_____

_____

List three things that you will do to help save and protect water.

Students' lists may vary. Most lists will reflect the suggestions given in the text.

_____

_____

_____

Name_____ Date_____

CARING FOR OUR WATER

What are some things that can happen to clean water?

Clean water can be polluted with hazardous chemicals, sewage, and trash, making it unsafe for humans to use.

How does water pollution move from place to place?

Streams and rivers carry water pollution to lakes and oceans. Ocean currents and tides move polluted ocean water from one place to another.

What are some ways you can conserve water?

Possible answers include repairing leaky faucets, not letting water run longer than necessary, operating dishwashers and washing machines only with full loads, and using devices to reduce water used in toilets.

What are some ways you can help keep water safe?

Possible answers include reducing the use of harmful chemicals and disposing of harmful chemicals in the proper way.

CHAPTER WRAP-UP

Name_____ Date_____

Think about what you learned in Chapter 3 when you answer the following questions.

1. What is something new you learned from this chapter about water pollution?

Answers will vary. Some students might discuss how water pollution moves from place to place. Others might mention the causes of water pollution.

_____

_____

2. Now what do you think about the importance of having clean water?

Most students will state that people must have clean water for drinking and other uses, so it is very important to keep water safe.

_____

_____

3. How did this chapter help you understand your responsibility in saving and protecting water?

Students might suggest that they learned there are steps they can take to conserve water and protect it from pollution.

_____

_____

4. What is something you learned in this chapter that you will share with your family?

Answers will vary. Many students will share some of the ways to save and protect water with their families.

_____

_____

UNIT
D

Name_____ Date_____

UNIT PROJECT WRAP-UP

Think about your model of Waterville and the plan you helped design for this town's water system. What do you think are the best parts of the plan?

Answers may vary. Students should identify what they think will work best in the
water system they helped plan.

_____

_____

What parts of the plan do you think could be improved?

Answers will vary. Students should identify parts of their water system plan that
could be improved.

_____

_____

How did this model help you learn about how you get clean drinking water?

Students might state that the model helped them learn about how water is treated
to make it safe and delivered to homes.

_____

_____

How did your model teach others about saving and protecting water?

Students will probably mention that the calendar they designed for Waterville
explains what people can do to conserve water and help reduce water pollution.

_____

_____

UNIT E

Name_____ Date_____

ROLES OF LIVING THINGS

In Unit E you'll learn how living things are adapted to live in their environments and their roles in those environments. For the Unit Project Big Event, you will hold a Rain Forest Celebration Day for which you will study the roles of plants and animals that live in rain forests. Describe what you think the environment of a rain forest is like.

Students might describe a rain forest as being a very warm place throughout the year with lots of rainfall.

_____

_____

What role might plants play in the rain forest environment?

Students might suggest that plants provide animals with food, shelter, and protection. Plants also provide other plants with a place to live. Some students may suggest that plants, by trapping the Sun's energy, form the basis for all food chains.

_____

_____

What role do you think animals have in the rain forest?

Students might suggest that animals consume plants and other animals, and provide food for other animals.

_____

_____

How do you think people affect the rain forest?

Students might explain that some people destroy the environment by clearing all the trees so the land can be farmed. Other people try to preserve the rain forest environment by helping to conserve rain forest resources.

_____

_____

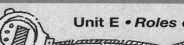

Name_____ Date_____

UNIT PREVIEW
....

Consider what you already know about living things. What would you like to learn about the roles they have in their environments? Write your ideas on the lines below.

_____

_____

_____

_____

_____

_____

_____

_____

_____

_____

_____

Name_____ Date_____

RELATIONSHIPS AMONG LIVING THINGS

Draw what a bird needs to survive.

Students' drawings should include a source of water, food (insects and worms), and trees (for shelter). They should also show that the environment is warm.

Use with pages E4–E5.

Name _____ Date _____

Dear Journal,

Plants and animals need these things to survive . . .

Some students might know that living things need food, water, air, and shelter.

_____

_____

Animals eat these kinds of foods . . .

Students might know that some animals eat only other animals, some animals eat only
plants, and some animals eat both plants and animals.

_____

_____

Plants get their food like this . . .

Some students might know that plants can make their own food.

_____

_____

I think that a food chain is . . .

Some students might know that a food chain is the path through which energy passes as
one living thing eats another. It begins with a plant and ends with a predator animal.

_____

_____

_____

ACTIVITY RECORD

CHAPTER **1**

Name_____ Date_____

NEEDS OF SEEDS

Procedure

Write your prediction for which conditions will be best for plant growth.

Students might predict that plants need water, soil, and sunlight for growth.

_____

In the chart below, **record your observations** of the plants after they have grown in their cups for one week.

Conditions	Plants After One Week
Soil	Plant should die.
Soil + Water	Plant should be yellow.
Soil + Water + Sunlight	Plant should grow best.

Analyze and Conclude

Write the answers to the questions in your book on the lines below.

1. The plant that grew best was the one that had soil, water, and sunlight. The others lacked either sunlight or both water and sunlight.

_____

_____

2. Answers will vary. Students should infer that plants need soil, water, and sunlight to live and grow.

_____

_____

Name_____ Date_____

A PILL BUG'S HOME

Procedure

Write your prediction for whether the pill bugs will move toward the light or away from the light.

Some students might predict that the pill bugs will move away from light.

_____

Record your observations of where the pill bugs move when you shine a flashlight over half of the pan.

The pill bugs should move under the newspaper, away from the light.

_____

_____

_____

Write your prediction for whether the pill bugs will move toward a dry area or a wet area.

Some students might predict that pill bugs will move toward a wet area.

_____

Record your observations of where the pill bugs move when you sprinkle water on half of the paper towel.

The pill bugs should move toward the wet paper towels.

_____

_____

_____

ACTIVITY RECORD

Name_____ Date_____

Analyze and Conclude

Write the answers to the questions in your book on the lines below.

1. <u>Pill bugs prefer darkness over light and moistness over dryness.</u>
_____

_____

2. <u>Pill bugs need darkness and moistness in their home.</u>
_____

_____

3. <u>Students should predict that pill bugs would be found under logs, leaves, stones, or in</u>
other dark, damp places.

_____

INVESTIGATE FURTHER!

EXPERIMENT

Page E9

What are two ways you can vary the conditions
of an earthworm's environment?
**Students might suggest varying temperature, food,
light, or moisture.**

Predict the conditions that the earthworms will prefer.
Students might predict that earthworms will prefer a moist, dark, and warm environment.

Record your observations as you vary the conditions of
the earthworms' environment.
Students should observe that earthworms prefer a moist, dark, and warm environment.

Name_____ Date_____

INVESTIGATION 1
•••••••••••••••••••••••••••••••••••••••

1. You put on scuba gear and dive into the ocean. As you explore the underwater world, you see many different kinds of plants and animals. What needs might they have in common?

Students should indicate that the plant and animal life in an ocean needs water, light, and can tolerate salt.

_____

_____

2. What would happen to a plant or an animal if it didn't get most of the things it needed?

Students should realize that if a plant or animal didn't get most of the things it needs, it would die. An animal could perhaps move to another environment to try to get its needs met, but a plant could not.

_____

_____

Name a plant or animal that you know and then describe its environment.

Answers will vary depending on the plants or animals students identify. They should describe the environments as being water or land and give some specific characteristics of them.

_____

_____

_____

CHAPTER 1

Name_____ Date_____

MEAT AND POTATOES

Procedure

Write your prediction about whether most of the foods you eat come from plants or animals.

Some students will predict that they eat mainly plants, others will predict that they eat mostly animals.

Record in the chart the kinds of foods you eat for one week.

What I Eat	
Food	From Plant or Animal
The information students record will depend on individual diets.	

Analyze and Conclude

Write the answer to the question in your book on the lines below.

Most foods probably come from plants. Students may have predicted more animal foods than results showed.

Name_____ Date_____

A MENU FOR MOLDS

Procedure

Write your prediction about what will happen to the bread and the cheese in the bag after one week in a warm, dark place.

Some students might predict that mold will start growing on the foods.

In the space below, **make drawings** of what you observe on the foods after one week.

Students should draw different kinds of molds growing on the foods.

Write your description of how the foods have changed after one week.

The bread and cheese should be starting to break down. Different-colored molds should be growing on the foods.

ACTIVITY RECORD

CHAPTER 1

Name_____ Date_____

In the space below, **make drawings** of what you observe on the foods after two weeks.

Students should draw larger colonies of molds growing on the foods.

Write your description of how the foods have changed after two weeks.

The foods should be broken down even more, and the molds should be larger.

_____

_____

Analyze and Conclude

Write the answers to the questions in your book on the lines below.

1. The food was eaten by molds. _____

_____

2. Molds use once-living things for food. _____

_____

3. Students should predict that more of the bread and cheese would be eaten by the molds.

_____

Name_____ Date_____

INVESTIGATION 2

1. You're designing a park. You want to make sure the plants and animals in your park will have food. What are the different ways living things get food energy? What living things would you include in your park?

Students should indicate that plants get energy from sunlight, and that animals get energy from plants or other animals. Students should indicate that they would include a variety of plants and animals in their parks.

2. Could you and other animals live if there were no plants? Why or why not?

Students should realize that all animals depend on plants or other animals that eat plants for food.

Make a chart in which you give examples of producers and consumers, including herbivores, carnivores, and omnivores.

Students might set up their charts like this. Examples will vary, but could include those listed.

Producers	Consumers		
	Herbivores	Carnivores	Omnivores
any plant	prairie dogs iguanas caterpillar elephants	spiders insects worms cats snakes wolves	humans bears raccoons some mice some birds turtles

Name_____ Date_____

MAKING A FOOD-CHAIN MOBILE

Procedure

Make a list of four living things, beginning with a plant.

Students should begin their lists with a plant, then list an animal that eats the plant,
then list an animal that eats the first animal, then list an animal that eats the second
animal.

_____

_____

In the space below, **draw** pictures of the living things in your
food chain.

Students should place the plant at the bottom of the food chain.

Name_____ Date_____

Analyze and Conclude

Write the answers to the questions in your book on the lines below.

1. The producer should be the bottom picture of a plant._____

_____

2. The top three pictures of animals should be consumers._____

_____

_____

3. Food chains begin with producers._____

_____

_____

Name_____ Date_____

MORE LINKS IN THE FOOD CHAIN

Procedure

Diagram each food chain you have made.

Possible food chains include berries—mouse—snake—owl; nuts— chipmunk—owl; water plants—crayfish—big fish; water plants—small fish—big fish—bear; berries—bear.

Make a drawing of your food web in the space below.

Students should show in their drawings how the food chains are linked together to form a food web.

CHAPTER 1

ACTIVITY RECORD

Name_____ Date_____

Write your inference about what would happen to living things that eat the producers if there were no producers.

Students should infer that the living things that ate producers would die if there were no producers.

_____

Write your inference about what would happen to the other members of the food web if there were no producers. Explain your inference.

Students should infer that the other animals in the food web would die if there were no producers because the animals they eat would have died due to the lack of food.

_____

_____

Analyze and Conclude

Write the answers to the questions in your book on the lines below.

1. A food chain links one living thing to another. A food web can link one living thing to several other living things. A food web is formed from two or more food chains.

_____

_____

_____

2. Students should conclude that the animals would die off unless they could move to another place.

_____

_____

Name_____ Date_____

UNIT PROJECT LINK

What sources did you use to learn about the producers that
live in each layer of a tropical rain forest?

For each source used, students should list its name, author, and the relevant page
numbers.

_____

_____

What plants are found in the canopy of a tropical rain forest?

Most of the rain forest plants live in the canopy. These plants include very large
trees, vines, ferns, flowering plants, and epiphytes—plants that use other plants for
support.

_____

What plants are found in the understory layer of a tropical
rain forest?

Answers may include shade-tolerant trees and bushes.

_____

_____

What plants are found on the forest floor in tropical rain
forests?

In most cases, the forest floor is bare of plants because not enough sunlight filters
down to the forest floor through the thick canopy.

_____

_____

Share this information with your group.

Name_____ Date_____

INVESTIGATION 3

·······································

1. You visit a forest where many hawks have been dying. You find chemical waste from a nearby factory in the forest soil and stream. How could the chemicals be harming the hawk?

<u>Students should explain that the chemicals could be in the water, plants, and small</u> animals that hawks eat. With each rung up the food chain, a higher concentration of <u>the chemicals is found. Hawks, relatively large predators, ingest enough of the chemical</u> to kill them.

_____

_____

2. Think about the different things you eat and where they come from. Draw a diagram that shows you as part of a food web.

Students' drawings should reveal a clear understanding of the concepts of food chains and food webs.

Diagram a food chain made up of a rabbit, a snake, mold, an owl, and grass. Label the producer, the predators, the prey, and the decomposer.

Students should diagram the food chain as grass—rabbit—snake—owl—mold. The grass is the producer. The mold is the decomposer. The rabbit is prey for the snake. The snake is prey for the owl. The snake and the owl are both predators.

CHAPTER WRAP-UP

Name_____ Date_____

RELATIONSHIPS AMONG LIVING THINGS

What do living things need to survive?

Food, water, air, a suitable environment, sunlight, and soil

_____

How do living things get the food they need?

Plants make their own food using sunlight. Animals get their food by only eating other
animals (carnivores), by only eating plants (herbivores), or by eating both plants and animals
(omnivores). Decomposers feed on the remains of once-living things.

_____

_____

What is a food chain?

A food chain is the path that energy takes as one living thing eats another. All food chains
begin with plants (producers) and end with decomposers. Prey and predator animals
(consumers) are the middle links in the food chain.

_____

Explain how food webs show that living things depend on each
other to survive.

Many animals are connected to one another by the plants and animals they eat. If one
kind of plant or animal were to disappear, a large number of other animals would be in
danger of dying because they no longer had food to eat.

_____

_____

Name_____ Date_____

Think about what you learned in Chapter 1 when you answer the following questions.

1. Describe what interested you the most about the relationships among living things.

Answers will vary. Students should describe a particular point about the relationships among living things in food chains or food webs.

_____

_____

_____

_____

2. What is your role in the environment? Describe where you fit into the food chain.

Most students will define themselves as omnivores. (Some may be herbivores.) They should explain that they are consumers and predators. Some may point out that they could also be prey to other predators in the environment.

_____

_____

_____

_____

3. What else would you like to learn about the relationships among living things? Explain how you would find out about it.

Answers will vary. Students might suggest reading additional sources, observing living things around them, or speaking with a naturalist or a zoologist.

_____

_____

_____

_____

CHAPTER 2

Name_____ Date _____

How Living Things Are Adapted

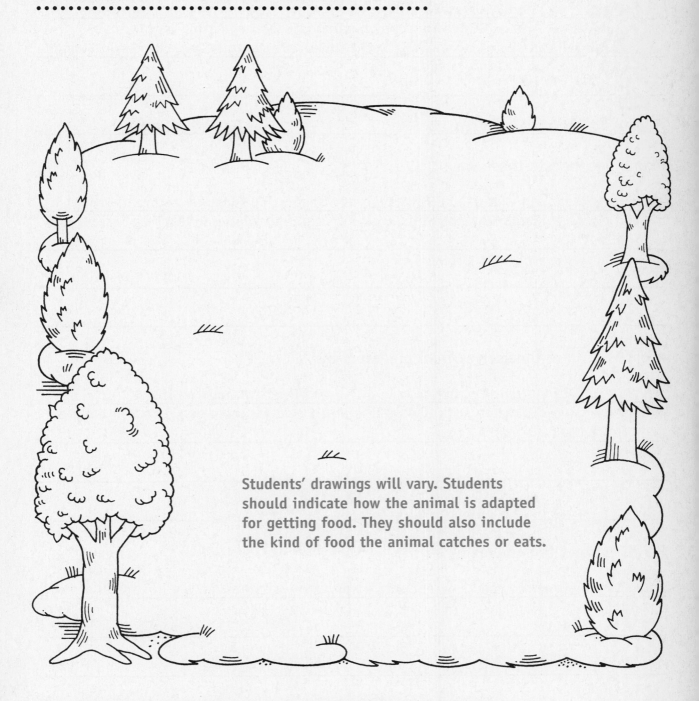

Students' drawings will vary. Students should indicate how the animal is adapted for getting food. They should also include the kind of food the animal catches or eats.

© Silver Burdett Ginn

Draw an animal and show how it's adapted for getting food.

Name_____ Date_____

Dear Journal,

I have seen animals get their food in these ways . . .

Answers will vary. Students might mention birds eating seeds or pulling worms from the
ground; horses or cows pulling up grass and eating it; rabbits gnawing on carrots or
leaves; squirrels holding an acorn while eating it; or an eagle catching a fish in its talons.

_____

_____

Plants get food in these ways . . .

Students will explain that plants make their own food using sunshine and nutrients from
the soil. Some students may know about plants, like venus flytraps, that trap insects for
nutrients.

_____

_____

Animals protect themselves from predators by . . .

Students might mention that animals can blend into their surroundings, have spines or
quills covering their bodies, look like other animals that are more dangerous, or behave
like they're dead.

_____

_____

Plants protect themselves by . . .

Students might mention that some plants have thorns or spines, have a bad taste, or are
poisonous.

_____

_____

_____

ACTIVITY RECORD

Name_____ Date_____

THE RIGHT BEAK FOR THE JOB

Procedure

Write your prediction for which bird beak is best for getting each kind of food.

Some students might predict that the toothpick is best for picking up the raisins. The taped fork is best for scooping up and filtering the rice grains. The spoon is best for scooping up the straw pieces.

In the chart below, **record** the total number of raisins, rice grains, and straw pieces that you pick up with each bird beak in ten tries.

Kind of Beak	Number of Raisins	Number of Rice Grains	Number of Straw Pieces
Toothpick	Numbers should represent total number of		
Fork	food pieces picked up in ten tries.		_____
Spoon	_____	_____	_____

Write your descriptions for the methods you used with the different beaks to pick up the different foods.

Students should describe stabbing with the toothpick, scooping and straining with the taped fork, and scooping with the spoon.

Analyze and Conclude

Write the answers to the questions in your book on the lines below.

1. Students should find that the toothpick is best for picking up the raisins, the fork with tape is best for picking up the pieces of rice, and the spoon is best for picking up the pieces of straw.

Name_____ Date_____

2. Students should infer that a bird that catches small animals buried in the mud or sand would have a pointy beak. Students should understand that for trapping small animals in shallow water a beak could be adapted to resemble a strainer. Students should infer that for catching fish in the deep ocean waters, a large, rounded beak that is used as a scoop would work best.

3. Students should conclude that birds with similar beaks eat the same types of food.

INVESTIGATE FURTHER!

RESEARCH

Page E39

List the names of the birds you plan to report on.

Students' lists will vary. Make sure students choose a variety of birds with different types of beaks.

Draw diagrams of the shape of each bird's beak you choose to study. Label each diagram with the name of the bird and the kind of food that bird eats.

Students should draw the beaks so that it is clear what kind of beak each bird has. Students should also label each beak with the name of the bird and the kind of food it eats.

Name_____ Date_____

INVESTIGATION 1
••••••••••••••••••••••••••••••

1. Think about an animal you often see outside. Write the name of the animal. What kind of food does the animal eat? What behaviors or body parts does the animal have for getting food?

Students may suggest a variety of organisms, including insects. Insects have mouth parts to help them obtain food, wings and six legs to help them get to food sources, and compound eyes to help them find food. They often live in social communities such as hives or colonies.

_____

_____

2. List three different animals or plants. For each, list an adaptation and explain how the adaptation is useful for getting food.

Responses may include grass (branching roots enable it to reach a lot of soil to absorb nutrients), a cow (flat teeth are adapted for chewing plant material), or a cat (claws help it capture prey.)

_____

Draw and label the parts of a bear that help it find and get food. Explain what each body part does.

Students should draw and label the eyes (help the bear see food), the nose (for smelling food), the ears (for hearing prey), the teeth (for biting and chewing food), and sharp claws (for catching prey and climbing trees to get food).

Name_____ Date_____

PLANT PROTECTION

Procedure

Draw your observations of the stem and leaves of a rose. Label the parts of the drawing you think are adaptations for protection.

Students should include the thorns on the rose stem and the sharp points around the leaves in their drawings. They should label these as being adaptations for protection.

Make a drawing of a holly leaf. Label the parts of the leaf you think are adaptations for protection.

In their drawings students should include the thorns at the ends of the points on the leaf. They should label these thorns as adaptations for protection.

ACTIVITY RECORD

Name_____ Date_____

Analyze and Conclude

Write the answer to the question in your book on the lines below.

Students should infer that animals would avoid eating a plant after finding that the
thorns are painful.

_____

_____

_____

_____

_____

Name_____ Date_____

PILL BUGS' DEFENSE
• •

Procedure

Record your observations of the pill bugs in the middle of the pan.

Students should record how the pill bugs look (pill bugs have a tough, outside covering
and a soft belly), and how they behave (at this point, the pill bugs should be uncurled.)

Write your prediction about what a pill bug will do when you
touch it.

Some students might predict that the pill bug will curl into a ball.

Record your observations of what happens when you touch the
pill bug.

The pill bug should curl into a ball.

Write your prediction about how the pill bugs will behave when
you add some vinegar to one side of the pan.

Some students might predict that the pill bugs will move away from the vinegar.

Record your observations as you add some vinegar to the pan.

The pill bugs should move away from the vinegar.

Analyze and Conclude

Write the answers to the questions in your book on the lines below.

1. Pill bugs curl into balls when touched. Students should infer that the tough, outside
covering protects the bugs' soft belly from attack by a predator.

2. Pill bugs crawl away from vinegar drops. Students should infer that since vinegar is
acidic, pill bugs will also run away from poisons they may encounter.

CHAPTER 2

Name_____ Date_____

BLENDING IN
....

Procedure

Record where you plan to hide your insect.

Students should describe some place or area in the classroom.

_____

List the colors, shapes, or patterns of this area that will help
your insect blend in with its surroundings.

Students should list the colors, shapes, or patterns of their places of choice that they can
use to make their insect blend in.

_____

_____

In the space below, **draw a diagram** of the insect you think will
blend in with the colors and shapes of the hiding place in your
classroom.

Students should draw an insect of any shape and color that would blend into a place in
the classroom. The insect should have six legs, 3 body segments, and wings.

Name_____ Date_____

Write your prediction about where your insect will be hardest to find.

Students should predict that their insect will be hardest to find in the place they chose originally to hide their insects.

_____

Write your description about what your insect looks like in its hiding place.

Students should explain how well the insect blends in with its surroundings.

_____

_____

Analyze and Conclude

Write the answers to the questions in your book on the lines below.

1. Students should reason that the insect that took the longest time to find was the hardest to find. Most probably it blended in well with its surroundings.

_____

_____

2. The more an insect's characteristics matched the background, the better hidden it was. An insect that matched the color, pattern, and shape of its background would be nearly invisible.

_____

_____

3. Students should predict that an insect with no way to hide from predators would have to escape by moving faster than its enemies or needs another defense, like a stinger.

_____

_____

Name_____ Date_____

UNIT PROJECT LINK
· ·

List some rain forest animals that you have read about.

<u>Many insects live in rain forests. Most invertebrates are birds, monkeys, snakes, and</u>
<u>lizards.</u>

_____

_____

_____

_____

Which rain forest animals live in trees? Describe how they
are adapted to this environment.

<u>Most animals in rain forests live in trees, or at least spend a lot of time in trees.</u>
<u>These animals, including birds, monkeys, snakes, and lizards, rarely go to the</u>
<u>ground. Even large predators, such as jaguars and panthers, spend a lot of time in</u>
trees. These animals are adapted to living in trees by having sharp claws that help
<u>them cling to branches; tails that wrap around branches; feet with "fingers" that</u>
help them grasp branches; or suction pads on the bottom of their toes.

_____

_____

Which animals in the rain forest are predators? Which animals are their prey?

<u>Predators include monkeys, lizards, frogs, anteaters, and tapirs (which eat insects);</u>
snakes and large birds (eat smaller animals); and jaguars, ocelots, and panthers (eat
<u>small and large animals).</u>

_____

_____

Share this information with your group.

Name_____ Date_____

INVESTIGATION 2

1. Imagine you are walking through a forest to observe the animals that live there. Describe some of the adaptations the animals might have to protect themselves.

Students may describe methods for camouflage or copying other animals. They may also suggest teeth, claws, and methods of escape.

_____

_____

_____

2. What are two adaptations that plants may have to protect themselves?

Students may suggest poisons, bitter taste, or thorns.

_____

_____

_____

Make a chart to list some adaptations that plants and animals have for defense. Point out types of adaptations that both plants and animals share.

Animals have camouflage, teeth, claws, and various behaviors for escape. Both plants and animals can look like a more dangerous living thing, can be poisonous or taste bad, and can have thorns or quills.

CHAPTER WRAP-UP

Name_____ Date_____

How Living Things Are Adapted

······································

What are some special body parts that living things have for getting food?

Animals might have keen senses of smell, eyesight, or hearing; deadly weapons, such as sharp claws, poison fangs, or sticky tongues; tools, such as specially shaped beaks. Plants have roots and leaves; and some plants have insect traps.

_____

_____

What are some ways in which animals behave to get food?

Animals might use tools from the environment to gather or eat food; stalk their food; or have special ways of moving or catching their food.

_____

_____

How are animals adapted for protection?

Animal adaptations for protection include camouflage; spines or quills on animal bodies; harmless animals that look like harmful animals; and behaviors, such as rolling up into a ball, pretending to be hurt or dead, or losing a tail.

_____

_____

_____

How are plants adapted for protection?

Plant adaptations for protection include thorns, poisonous or irritating chemicals, and bitter taste.

_____

_____

CHAPTER WRAP-UP

Use with page E59.

Name_____ Date_____

Think about what you learned in Chapter 2 when you answer the following questions.

1. What plant or animal adaptation did you find to be the most interesting? Explain.

Answers will vary. Students should explain why they found a particular body part or behavior of a living thing to be interesting.

_____

_____

_____

_____

2. How are you adapted for getting food and for defending yourself?

Some adaptations for getting food include using tools to grow, gather, and hunt for food; and hands with fingers and thumbs. Some adaptations for defense include sharp fingernails and the ability to run quickly.

_____

_____

_____

3. What else would you like to know about how living things are adapted to get food and protect themselves? How would you find out about this?

Answers will vary. Students might suggest reading additional sources, observing animals or plants at the zoo or in the neighborhood, or talking with a zoologist or naturalist.

_____

_____

_____

_____

Name_____ Date_____

LIVING THINGS IN THE ENVIRONMENT

Draw how you think this environment will look in 20 years.

Students' drawings will vary. Some may draw trees to make the field into a forest. Others may draw houses, shopping centers, or apartment buildings.

Name_____ Date_____

Dear Journal,

I have changed my environment in these ways . . .

Answers will vary. Students might mention gardening, helping to build a swing set or
other structure, littering, putting out bird feeders or bird houses, or planting a tree.

_____

_____

Animals change the environment in these ways . . .

Answers will vary. Students might mention birds building a nest, squirrels burying acorns,
beavers building a dam, rabbits digging a burrow, or ants building an ant hill.

_____

_____

_____

Animals have these kinds of adaptations to survive in the conditions of their environments . . .

Answers will vary. Students might suggest animals hibernating, or resting, during cold weather;
birds changing colors from winter to spring; birds and butterflies migrating during fall and
spring; or special body parts or behaviors to enable animals to live in extreme temperatures or
areas without much water.

_____

_____

Plants have these kinds of adaptations to live in the conditions
of their environments . . .

Answers might include losing leaves in fall, having needles as leaves, or having shallow
root systems.

_____

_____

_____

ACTIVITY RECORD

CHAPTER **3**

Name_____ Date_____

MY NEIGHBORHOOD KEEPS CHANGING!

Procedure

Make a list of all the changes you observe in the neighborhood pictured in your book.

Changes include a new home, a street, a sidewalk, a fence, a porch and new windows on the left house, an addition to the back of the right house, trees are larger.

Write your inference about who made the changes.

Students should infer that most of the changes were made by people.

Write your hypothesis about how the changes affected living things in the area.

Students might hypothesize that adding the street and sidewalks and building the house would have removed places for plants and animals to live. Growing a garden would give living things a new place to live.

Analyze and Conclude

Write the answers to the questions in your book on the lines below.

1. Human activities caused most changes. When the trees were cleared to build the house next door and sidewalks and streets were paved, mini-ecosystems would have been reduced or eliminated. The addition of a formal garden as well as birdbaths and bird feeders will create new homes and food supplies for some animals.

2. Answers might include people building more houses, stores, parks, or schools; adding new roads; cutting down or planting more trees; and existing trees will grow taller.

INVESTIGATE FURTHER!

TAKE ACTION

Page E63

Make a list of ideas for small changes that will improve the environment around your school.

Students might list picking up trash, putting up bird feeders or bird houses, planting a small garden, adding more trash cans to the school grounds, or planting a tree.

Choose one idea and **make a plan** to carry out the project.

Students should describe the steps required to complete their project, including getting permission to carry out the project, doing any research, getting supplies, building components, and carrying out the plan.

Infer how your project will affect living things.

Answers will vary depending on the plans. Students should explain how their plans will help living things by providing them with food or homes or by making their environment safer.

INVESTIGATION CLOSE

Name_____ Date_____

INVESTIGATION 1
· ·

1. You are a scientist exploring a tropical rain forest. You observe that a large part of the forest has been cut down. How might such a change affect the living things in that area? Explain your answer.

The trees and small plants that grow on the forest floor are gone. The animals, birds, and insects that depended on them for homes, protection from predators, and food might die or be forced to go live someplace else.

_____

_____

2. Explain three ways living things change the environment. Your examples can include changes made by people, other animals, or plants.

Possible answers: people can cut down trees, dig or fill ponds, dam rivers, build houses and roads, kill animals, and so on; beavers can build dams that form ponds and provide homes for other animals; buffalo and other animals can change land by grazing; plants can offer protection and food, thus attracting animals to an environment.

_____

_____

Make a flow chart that shows how the environment is affected when someone plants a tree.

Flow charts could look something like this.

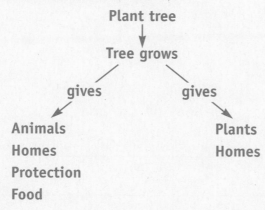

Name_____ Date_____

KEEPING HEAT IN
· ·

Procedure

Write your prediction for which animal model will lose more heat; the model with feathers or the one without.

Some students will predict that the animal model without feathers will lose more heat._____

_____

In the chart below, **record** the temperature of the water in each jar every 15 minutes.

Time (in min.)	Temperature (°C) Model With Feathers	Temperature (°C) Model Without Feathers
0	_____ The water temperature for the model with _____ feathers should stay warmer.	
15	_____	_____
30	_____	_____

Analyze and Conclude

Write the answers to the questions in your book on the lines below.

1. Exact measurements will vary, but the temperature in the jar surrounded by feathers should change less than the temperature in the other jar.

_____

ACTIVITY RECORD

Name_____ Date_____

2. The animal model without feathers lost more heat. This should match student predictions.

_____

_____

3. Feathers help a bird stay warm by holding in heat.

_____

_____

_____

Name_____ Date_____

UNIT PROJECT LINK
....

Make a list of resources that are found in rain forests.

<u>Answers might include minerals, hardwood timber, medicines, food, fuel, and fiber.</u>
<u>The rain forest also stabilizes Earth's climate by producing much of the world's oxygen,</u>
<u>filtering rain, and retaining the moisture needed for sufficient rainfall for all of</u>
<u>Earth. The rain forest is also home to more plants and animals than any other place</u>
<u>in the world, and many of these living things haven't been identified yet.</u>

_____

_____

What are some reasons why the tropical rain forest is disap-
pearing?

<u>Answers might include rain forests are cleared so that farm crops can be grown and</u>
<u>farm animals can be raised. Since the soil is poor, it can't support crops for long, so</u>
<u>more of the forest is destroyed to start new farms.</u>

_____

_____

Make a list of ideas that you could use on a poster that
describes what people can do to help save the rain forests.

<u>Answers will vary. Some ways to conserve rain forests include purchasing products</u>
<u>designed to conserve rain forest resources and not purchasing hardwood timber that</u>
<u>is found only in rain forests.</u>

_____

_____

_____

Share this information with your group.

INVESTIGATION 2
....

1. You walk through a forest. There is snow on the ground and on tree branches and bushes. You see only one or two kinds of birds. What adaptation do the birds have for keeping warm? Why did other kinds of birds leave?

These birds have feathers to decrease heat loss. The other birds have feathers, too, but they may eat food that is not available in winter, such as insects. They have adapted to the cold by migrating to more favorable environments.

2. What adaptation do you have to beat the heat? Do most desert animals have the same adaptation? Explain your answer.

People perspire in the heat, using the drying process to cool their skin. Desert animals can't perspire, because they would dry up and die without new water sources to replenish them. Other human strategies are to use air conditioning, drink lots of water, wear lighter weight clothes, and so on. Some desert animals, such as the kangaroo rat, can actually air-condition their burrows by plugging up the entrance so it remains cool. Desert animals cannot drink lots of water, but must find ways to conserve what moisture they have because their water supply is usually very limited.

Draw a diagram showing how a maple tree is adapted to live through cold winters.

Students should draw a tree with leaves, then a tree without leaves to show that maple trees lose their leaves so they can survive through cold winters.

Name_____ Date_____

LIVING THINGS IN THE ENVIRONMENT

How can plants and animals change the environment?

Answers might include beavers building dams that create ponds; buffalo and other animals eating plants; and plants growing and providing homes and food for animals.

How can people change the environment?

Answers might include building streets, housing, stores; farming, draining wetlands, digging lakes, creating parks, and planting trees and gardens.

How are living things adapted to very hot, dry environments?

Some insects are covered with a light-colored waxy coating. Animals don't lose water by sweating or urinating and can get water from their food. Animals are only active at night when it's cooler and sleep during the hot day. Plants store water inside themselves and have thin, spiny leaves that don't lose water.

How are living things adapted to the cycles of summer and winter in the environment?

Some animals migrate, others hibernate. Some plants lose their leaves; others die above ground, but their roots survive underground.

CHAPTER WRAP-UP

Name_____ Date_____

Think about what you learned in Chapter 3 when you answer the
following questions.

1. What was the most surprising thing you learned about living
things and their environments?

Answers will vary. Students might describe an adaptation of a living thing to help it
survive or a way in which a living thing can change its environment.

_____

_____

2. What did you learn about the importance of the role of people
and their effects on the environment?

Answers will vary. Students might describe how people have the ability to change the
environment in ways that could harm or help other living things.

_____

_____

3. What ideas about living things and their environment did you
already know about?

Answers will vary. Some students might have known why animals migrate and hibernate,
or how some animals can change the environment.

_____

_____

4. What else would you like to know about living things and the
environment? How would you find out about it?

Answers will vary. Students might suggest reading additional sources, observing living
things in their environments, or speaking with a naturalist or zoologist.

_____

_____

_____

Name_____ Date_____

UNIT PROJECT WRAP-UP
· ·

Think about your Rain Forest Celebration Day. What part did
you like the best? Explain.

<u>Students should explain which part of their project they liked best—the rain forest</u>
mural, the jungle talks, or the "Save the Rain Forest" posters.

_____

_____

What did you learn about the rain forest environment by
creating the rain forest mural?

<u>Students might explain that by creating the mural, they learned about the adapta-</u>
tions of the living things in the rain forest and what their roles are.

_____

_____

What did you describe in your jungle talk? Why did you
choose to talk about this subject?

<u>Answers will vary. Students should explain the topic they discussed in their jungle</u>
talk and why they chose to talk about that topic.

_____

_____

How does your poster show people that they have an effect
on the rain forest environment, even though they may live
far away from a rain forest?

<u>Answers will vary. Students might explain that by purchasing or not purchasing certain</u>
products, then rain forest resources can be conserved.

_____

_____

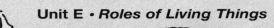

Roles of Living Things • Unit E

Name_____ Date_____

WHAT'S FOR LUNCH?

In Unit F you'll learn about nutrients, healthful diets, handling food safely, and digestion. For the Unit Project Big Event, you'll use everything you've learned to create and display a food pyramid supermarket. You'll also prepare healthful menus based on the recommended daily servings of foods from each food group.

What should be included in a healthful diet?

Some students might suggest that a good mixture of cereals and grains, fruits, vegetables, meat, and milk products make up a healthful diet.

_____

_____

_____

Why is it important to eat healthful foods? Explain why your body needs food.

Healthful foods give the body the nutrients it needs for energy, growth, and repair.

_____

_____

_____

How does your body get the things it needs from food?

Through the process of digestion, the body breaks down food into the nutrients that the body needs.

_____

_____

_____

Name_____ Date_____

UNIT PREVIEW
....

Everyone knows about food. We all need food to live. How
much do you know about nutrients and what makes a
healthful diet? What would you like to learn? List your ideas
on the lines below.

_____

_____

_____

_____

_____

_____

_____

_____

_____

_____

_____

Name_____ Date_____

THE FOODS WE EAT

Draw foods that would make up a healthful meal.

Students' drawings will vary. A healthful meal should include foods that are low in fat, sugar, and salt. Foods like cereal and grains, fruits, vegetables, meats, and milk products all make up a healthful meal.

Name_____ Date_____

Dear Journal,

My body uses food for these things . . .

Some students might know that the body uses food for growth, healing wounds, and energy.

_____

_____

My body uses these nutrients from food . . .

Some students might know that the body uses carbohydrates, fats, proteins, water, vitamins, and minerals from food.

_____

_____

These kinds of foods are healthful foods . . .

Students might list breads and cereals, fruits, vegetables, milk products, and meats.

_____

_____

These kinds of foods are not healthful foods . . .

Students might list fats, sweets, salty foods, and oils.

_____

_____

Food should be stored and handled in these ways . . .

Students might know that most food should be stored in the refrigerator or freezer, everything touching food should be kept clean, and foods should be cooked thoroughly.

_____

_____

Name_____ Date_____

PUT IT TO THE TEST

Procedure

In the chart below, **record** the foods that you will be testing for starch. Then **write your predictions** for which foods will turn iodine black.

Test for Starch

Kind of Food	Prediction	Color of Iodine Spot	Does It Contain Starch?
potato	Predictions may	black	yes
cheese	or may not be	varies	no
apple	accurate.	varies	no
bread		black	yes
cooked noodle		black	yes

Record your observations as you test each food for starch. Then **record** whether the foods contain starch.

Analyze and Conclude

Write the answers to the questions in your book on the lines below.

1. The potato, bread, and noodle contain starch; the cheese and apple do not.

2. Bread, pasta, and potatoes

3. Knowing which nutrients that foods provide helps you plan meals that include a variety of nutrients.

Name_____ Date_____

FINDING FAT

Procedure

In the chart below, **record** the names of each food you will test for fat. **Write your predictions** for which foods will have fat in them.

Test for Fat

Kind of Food	Prediction	Grease Spot	Does It Contain Fat?
potato chip	Predictions may	yes	yes
cheese	or may not be	yes	yes
butter cookie	accurate.	yes	yes
raw carrot		no	no
raw potato		no	no
bologna		yes	yes

Record the results of your test for fat. Then **record** whether each food contains fat.

Analyze and Conclude

Write the answers to the questions in your book on the lines below.

1. The potato chip, cheese, butter cookie, and bologna contained fat, as shown by the grease spots.

_____

2. The potato slice did not leave a grease spot; the potato chip did. Potato chips are cooked in fat.

_____

3. If you know which foods contain fat, you can avoid them if you're trying to cut down on fat.

_____

INVESTIGATE FURTHER

Name_____ Date_____

INVESTIGATE FURTHER!
EXPERIMENT
Page F9

Make a list below of snack foods that you will test for fat. **Write your predictions** for which foods will contain fat.

Food	Prediction	Grease Spot?
dry cereals	Predictions may	no
crackers	or may not be	some will
cookies	accurate.	most will
pastries		most will
fresh fruits		no
nuts		yes

Record the results of the fat test for each food.

Which foods would you avoid if you were trying to cut down on fat?

Students should list the snack foods that contain fat; those that left a grease spot on the brown paper.

INVESTIGATE FURTHER!
EXPERIMENT
Page F13

Make a list of all the foods you eat in one day.

Some possible answers include cereal—carbohydrate; milk—protein; juice—carbohydrate; bread—carbohydrate; peanut butter—protein; jelly—carbohydrate; apple—carbohydrate; cheese stick—fat.

Record the nutrients in each food on your list.

Which nutrient do you eat most during a day?

Most students will eat more carbohydrates than proteins or fats.

Name_____ Date_____

INVESTIGATION 1
....

1. Some people take vitamins every day, though many doctors
say this isn't necessary. Based on what you've learned, who
should take vitamins and who probably doesn't need to?

Vitamins may be needed by people who don't eat enough of a variety of foods, who are
ill, or whose bodies need extra vitamins. Most people should not need extra vitamins if
they eat a well-balanced diet with many unprocessed foods.

_____

_____

2. List the six nutrients found in food. Tell why your body needs
each one.

The six nutrients are carbohydrates, fats, proteins, water, vitamins, and minerals.
Carbohydrates: energy; fats: energy, help body use vitamins, keep body warm, cushion
joints; proteins: build body parts for growth, repair injured body parts, control body
functions, fight disease; water: removes waste, required in body processes, controls
body temperature; vitamins: trigger body functions, help clot blood, help release energy
from other nutrients; minerals: make up bones and teeth, control amount of body fluids,
trigger body functions.

_____

_____

List one source of food for each of the six kinds of nutrients.

Answers will vary. Possible answers include carbohydrates: fruits, vegetables, breads, and
cereals; fats: oil, cheese, butter, and meat; proteins: milk, eggs, fish, nuts; water: water,
fruits, vegetables; vitamins: citrus fruits, milk, carrots; minerals: bananas, broccoli, citrus
fruits.

_____

_____

Name_____ Date_____

RATE YOUR DIET
....

Procedure

Write your prediction about how healthful your diet is.

Many students will predict that their diets are healthful.

Record in the chart below everything you eat for the next three days.

Meal	Day 1	Day 2	Day 3
Breakfast	Students should list in detail everything they eat.		
Lunch			
Dinner			
Snacks			

Name_____ Date_____

Record your thoughts about whether the foods you eat are providing you with all the nutrients you need.

Students should decide which nutrients they need to include more or less of in their diets.

_____

_____

Analyze and Conclude

Write the answers to the questions in your book on the lines below.

1. Students will be able to tell on which day they had the most nutrients by comparing their charts to the one on page F10.

_____

2. Foods that are lowest in nutrients probably include snacks containing a lot of sugar and fat.

_____

3. Student answers should accurately rate the healthfulness of their diets and compare them with their predictions.

_____

_____

_____

4. Student paragraphs should include such improvements as drinking more water, eating more fruits and vegetables, eating more starches, and eating less sugar and fat.

_____

_____

_____

_____

INVESTIGATION CLOSE

Name_____ Date_____

INVESTIGATION 2
....

1. Use the Food Guide Pyramid on page F19 to plan a menu for
one day. Your menu should include the recommended number
of servings of all five food groups.

Students' menus should include no more than one or two items from the fats, sweets,
and oil group.

_____

_____

_____

2. List your five favorite snacks. Which ones are healthful? Think
of a healthful snack to replace each snack from the fats,
sweets, and oils group.

Healthful snacks may include fruit, vegetables, and other healthful foods from the
food groups.

_____

_____

_____

_____

Draw a pie chart that shows the amounts of fats, proteins, and carbohydrates needed for a healthful diet. For each nutrient, write the
food group from the Food Guide Pyramid that provides that nutrient.

Pie charts should look similar to the one on page F18. The bread, cereal, rice, and pasta
group; the fruit group; and the vegetable group provide carbohydrates. The meat and milk
groups provide proteins and fats.

Name_____ Date_____

How Sweet It Is!
....

Procedure

Write your prediction for how much sugar is in each cereal by listing the cereals in order from the cereal with the most sugar the one with the least sugar.

Students should list the cereals in order from the one they predict has the most sugar to the one they predict has the least sugar.

_____

_____

In the chart below, **record** the cereals in the order you predicted, from the most sugar to the least sugar.

Cereal Data		
Cereal	Does It Contain Sugar? What Kinds?	Where Is Sugar on the Ingredient List?
	Ingredient lists might include variations of the kinds of sugars listed in the chart.	Each sugar listed should have a place number on the ingredient list.

Record in the chart the kinds of sugars in each cereal. Then for each cereal **record** the place number for each sugar on the ingredient list.

ACTIVITY RECORD

CHAPTER 1

Name_____ Date_____

Analyze and Conclude

Write the answers to the questions in your book on the lines below.

1. Answers should indicate the cereal with the most sugar and whether or not their predictions were accurate.

_____

_____

2. Answers will depend on the cereals used in the activity.

_____

_____

3. Students will be able to choose cereals that have little sugar.

_____

_____

Name_____ Date_____

CHECK THE LABEL

Procedure

In the chart below, **list** the names of the foods you will be studying. Then **record** the number of Calories in one serving of each food.

| Food | Nutrition Facts | | | |
	Calories in One Serving	Amount of Fat and Saturated Fat	Amount of Cholesterol	Amount of Salt (sodium)
Data will depend on the food labels students study. Students should study at least four different food labels.				

For each food **record** the amounts of fat, saturated fat, and cholesterol listed on the food label. Then, **record** the amount of sodium in one serving of each food.

ACTIVITY RECORD

Name_____ Date_____

Analyze and Conclude

Write the answers to the questions in your book on the lines below.

1. Answers will depend on the foods chosen. Foods high in saturated fat will also be high in cholesterol.

2. Foods high in fat and sugar will be high in Calories.

3. Foods high in fat, sodium, and cholesterol should be rated *Not Recommended,* and those low in these nutrients should be rated *Highly Recommended*.

INVESTIGATE FURTHER!
....
EXPERIMENT

Page F27

Record the suggested serving size for the cereal you chose to study.

Students should record the suggested serving size given in the Nutrition Facts label on the box of cereal.

Compare the suggested serving size of the cereal with the amount of cereal you usually eat.

Most students will eat more cereal in one serving than the suggested serving size given on the box.

Calculate the amount of fat, cholesterol, and sodium in your usual serving of cereal.

Students should measure their usual serving size of cereal. Then use ratios to determine the amount of fat, sodium, and cholesterol in their usual serving of cereal. Most students will be getting more fat, cholesterol, and sodium because their usual serving size is larger than the suggested serving.

Name_____ Date_____

UNIT PROJECT LINK
....

In the space below, list as many healthful foods as you can.
Tell which food group each food belongs to.

Lists should include foods that are low in sugar, sodium, and fat. Next to each food
listed, students should write the food group to which it belongs.

_____

_____

_____

_____

_____

_____

Choose foods from your list to make a menu for all the meals
and snacks that you would eat in one day. Give the serving
size for each food, as suggested in the Food Guide Pyramid.

Students should indicate what foods would be eaten for each meal—breakfast,
lunch, and dinner; and what foods would be eaten as snacks.

_____

_____

_____

_____

_____

Share this information with your group.

INVESTIGATION CLOSE

Name_____ Date_____

INVESTIGATION 3
· ·

1. Write down your favorite fast-food meal. What servings from the food pyramid would it count for? What would you have to eat the rest of the day to get all the servings that you need?

Student responses will probably show high levels of fat, salt, and sugar in the fast-food meal. Other meals for the day would need to include fruits, vegetables, some protein, and starches.

_____

_____

2. Explain how food labels can help you make wise food choices. What kinds of foods should you avoid?

Food labels provide information about nutrition. Foods to be avoided include those high in fats, salts, and sugars.

_____

_____

Make up a food label for a healthful food and a junk food.

Students should include the serving size for each food and the number of Calories per serving. They should also give the amounts of fats, carbohydrates, sugar, and sodium for each food. The healthful food should have less fat, sugar, and sodium than the junk food.

Name_____ Date_____

TATER TROUBLE

Procedure

Write your predictions about how the potato slice in each bag
will look after one week.

Bag *A* Some students might predict that the potato rubbed with their unwashed hands

will start to rot.

Bag *B* Some students might predict that the potato placed in the bag with gloved hands

will not change very much.

Bag *C* Some students might predict that the potato rubbed on the floor will start to rot.

Record your descriptions of the potato slice in each bag after
being stored in a warm place for one week.

Bag *A* The potato slice will probably be black and have mold growing on it. There might

also be some liquid in the bag.

Bag *B* The potato slice might be black, but it should have changed less than the potato

slice in Bag *A*.

Bag *C* The potato slice will probably look similar to or worse than the potato slice in

Bag *A*.

ACTIVITY RECORD

CHAPTER 1

Name_____ Date_____

Analyze and Conclude

Write the answers to the questions in your book on the lines below.

1. The degree of contact with dirt, or germs, caused the differences.

_____

_____

2. It is important to wash your hands because there are more germs on your hands when they are dirty and germs can move from your hands to food.

_____

_____

_____

Name_____ Date_____

INVESTIGATION 4
· ·

1. Imagine that you open a can of soup and notice that the soup doesn't look or smell right. Describe what you would do.

Students should not taste the soup. They should tell an adult who should contact the
store where the can was purchased.

_____

_____

2. Explain why it's important to keep everything that touches food clean when handling food. What are some rules you should follow to keep foods safe to eat?

Student responses should include that bacteria are everywhere and can grow in foods if
the foods aren't handled properly. Students should list some of the rules from the
table Keeping Food Clean as well as thawing foods in the refrigerator, eating only fully
cooked meat and eggs, refrigerating leftovers right away, and keeping hot foods hot
and cold foods cold when serving.

_____

_____

Make a word web to show different ways to keep foods fresh.

Students should show that refrigeration, freezing, and freeze-drying keep foods fresh by
cooling them. Pasteurization and canning keep foods fresh by using heat. Smoking, salt-
ing, and irradiation are other ways of keeping food fresh.

Name_____ Date_____

THE FOODS WE EAT

Why does your body need food?

The body needs food for energy, growth, and repair.

What parts of food does your body need?

The body uses the nutrients from food. These nutrients are carbohydrates, proteins, fats, water, vitamins, and minerals.

What food groups are part of a healthful diet?

The food groups in the Food Guide Pyramid that are part of a healthful diet include the bread, cereal, rice, and pasta group; the fruit group; the vegetable group; the milk group; and the meat group. Fats and oils are necessary for good health, but most often can be obtained as components of other food groups.

How do food labels help you choose healthful foods?

Food labels give the amounts of Calories, fat, cholesterol, sodium, carbohydrate, sugars, protein, vitamins, and minerals per serving of food in the package. By knowing what nutrients are in foods, it's possible to choose between foods that are healthful and those that aren't.

How can you keep food safe to eat?

Control the temperature at which food is stored and served, make sure food is thoroughly cooked, and keep everything that touches food clean.

CHAPTER WRAP-UP

Name_____ Date_____

Think about what you learned in Chapter 1 when you answer the following questions.

1. What did you find most interesting about the foods you eat?

Answers will vary. Some students might have been most interested in the food labels or in the food pyramid.

_____

_____

2. How will you use what you've learned about nutrients in foods?

Students might mention that they will eat more healthful diets by choosing healthful foods and avoiding foods high in fat, sugar, and salt.

_____

_____

3. What was the most difficult idea for you to understand about foods and nutrition? Tell how you can help yourself understand it better.

Answers will vary. Some students might find the food label confusing or have trouble remembering what the nutrients provide. Students might suggest rereading the chapter, redoing some activities, or asking questions.

_____

_____

4. What else would you like to know about the foods you eat? How could you find out about this?

Answers will vary. Students might suggest reading additional sources or talking with a food nutritionist.

_____

_____

_____

Name_____ Date_____

HOW THE BODY USES FOOD

Students' drawings will vary. They should include the mouth, tongue, and teeth in their drawings as well as the throat, stomach, and intestines.

Think about how food travels through your body after you eat it. Draw what you think your digestive system looks like.

Name_____ Date_____

Dear Journal,

When I eat food, digestion begins . . .

Some students might know that chewing food in the mouth begins the digestive process.

_____

_____

After swallowing, food travels to these parts of the body to be
digested . . .

Students might know that after swallowing, food moves into the stomach, then into the
small intestine, and finally into the large intestine.

_____

_____

After food has been digested, these things happen to the nutrients from the food . . .

Some students might know that nutrients enter the bloodstream from the small intestine
and are carried to cells in the body where they are used for energy, growth, and repair.

_____

_____

_____

I take care of my teeth by . . .

Possible answers include brushing, flossing, and visiting the dentist regularly.

_____

_____

ACTIVITY RECORD

CHAPTER 2

Name_____ Date_____

A MATTER OF TASTE

Procedure

In the chart below, **record** the name of each food you taste under the heading where you think it belongs.

Salty	Sweet	Sour	Bitter
Some examples include the following.			
pretzels	sugar	lemons	bitter chocolate
salt	cookies	sour candy	grapefruit rind

In the chart below, **record** whether or not you identify each of the grated foods correctly when you taste them while holding your nose.

Grated Food	What You Thought It Was	Identified Correctly?
Apple	Most students will not identify the foods correctly.	
Pear		
Potato		

CHAPTER 2

Name_____ Date_____

Analyze and Conclude

Write the answers to the questions in your book on the lines below.

1. Students should be able to identify the four distinct tastes—salty, sweet, sour, and bitter—and place different foods in the correct categories.

_____

_____

_____

2. Most students should not be able to identify the foods while they hold their noses. They should infer that the sense of smell enhances taste.

_____

_____

3. Students should recall that foods taste bland when they have a cold; they should infer that a congested nose diminishes the sense of taste.

_____

_____

_____

Name_____ Date_____

 # INVESTIGATION 1
....

1. How does chewing make it easier for saliva to begin breaking down food with chemicals?

When food is chewed into small pieces, the chemicals in saliva can break it down more easily.

2. What is digestion? List the steps of digestion that take place in the mouth. Then briefly describe what happens to food in the first and second stages of swallowing.

Digestion is the physical and chemical breakdown of food into a form the body can use. Students' lists should include releasing saliva, breaking food into pieces, and mashing food against the palate. In the first stage of swallowing the back part of the palate rises up and closes off the nasal passage, the tongue pushes food to the back of the throat, and the flap of skin closes off the windpipe. In the second stage of swallowing, the throat muscles squeeze the food to the top of the esophagus.

Make a chart that shows which steps of digestion in the mouth are chemical digestion and which are physical digestion.

Students should show that the biting, cutting, tearing, and grinding actions of teeth; the movements of the tongue; and the moistening of food by saliva are physical digestion. They should show that saliva breaking down starch into sugar is chemical digestion.

Name_____ Date_____

CHEW ON THIS

Procedure

Draw the shape of each kind of tooth you see in your mouth.

Students should draw pictures of at least three different kinds of teeth—incisors (sharp teeth), canines (pointed teeth), and molars (bumpy teeth).

Write your inferences about how each kind of tooth works when you eat.

Some students will infer that the incisors (sharp teeth) bite food, the canines (pointed teeth) tear food, and the molars (bumpy teeth) crush and grind food.

_____

_____

Record your observations of how each kind of tooth works as you eat a celery stick.

Students should observe that the incisors (sharp teeth) bite food, the canines (pointed teeth) tear food, and the molars (bumpy teeth) crush and grind food.

_____

_____

ACTIVITY RECORD

Name_____ Date_____

Analyze and Conclude

Write the answers to the questions in your book on the lines below.

1. You have sharp teeth for biting food, pointed teeth for tearing it, and bumpy teeth for crushing and grinding it.

_____

_____

2. You would be able to eat only very soft foods and liquids.

_____

_____

_____

CHAPTER 2

Name_____ Date_____

A TOOTHY PROBLEM

Procedure

Write your prediction about how easy or hard it will be to get all the peanut butter off the comb.

Some students might predict that it will be hard to get all the peanut butter off the comb.

_____

Record your results after rinsing the peanut-butter-covered comb with water.

The comb will still have a lot of peanut butter on it.

_____

Record your results after brushing the comb with a toothbrush.

Most of the peanut butter will be removed. There will probably be some in the small spaces between the teeth of the comb.

_____

Record your results after flossing the teeth of the comb.

The comb shouldn't have any peanut butter left on it.

_____

Analyze and Conclude

Write the answers to the questions in your book on the lines below.

1. Students might have predicted that it would be easy to remove the peanut butter from the comb. They may have found it harder than they predicted.

_____

_____

ACTIVITY RECORD

Name_____ Date_____

2. Rinsing removed the big chunks of peanut butter, brushing removed most of the rest, and flossing was needed to remove peanut butter from the smallest areas.

_____

_____

3. Students might suggest that the best way to clean their teeth would be to rinse, brush, and then floss.

_____

_____

INVESTIGATE FURTHER!

RESEARCH

Page F53

How are dentists using lasers in their work?

Dentists use lasers to remove or treat soft gum tissue, kill bacteria between teeth and gums, and remove plaque. Some day soon, they may also use lasers instead of drilling.

Is your dentist using lasers in his or her work? Describe what your dentist uses lasers for.

Not all dentists are currently using lasers in their work. Some might use lasers for only one procedure such as removing plaque, and others might use lasers for many different procedures.

Name_____ Date_____

INVESTIGATION 2

1. What can happen to teeth if too many bacteria grow in your mouth?

Too much bacteria will cause teeth to decay and loosen from the gums. Bacteria also causes gum disease and bad breath.

_____

_____

2. List the steps for having healthy teeth. Explain why healthy teeth are important.

Brushing and flossing teeth after eating and visiting the dentist twice a year are actions students should note. They should realize that healthy teeth are important for proper nutrition.

_____

_____

Use a mirror to count the number of teeth in your mouth. Then draw a diagram of your mouth showing the location of each tooth.

Most 3rd graders (8-year-olds) have 24 teeth, assuming that no teeth are lost. Students should draw four incisors, two canines, four premolars, and two molars on the top gum, with the same number of teeth on the bottom gum. Drawings should also show where students have lost a baby tooth and are waiting for the permanent tooth to grow in.

ACTIVITY RECORD

CHAPTER 2

Name_____ Date_____

THE BIG BREAKDOWN

Procedure

In the chart below, **write your predictions** about whether or not glucose is present in each food.

Food	Glucose Present?	
	Prediction	Result
Apple juice	Predictions may or may not be accurate.	yes
Orange juice		yes
Cranberry juice		yes
Milk		no
Milk with lactase		yes

In the chart **record the results** of the glucose test for each food.

Analyze and Conclude

Write the answers to the questions in your book on the lines below.

1. The test strip should have darkened noticeably in the apple juice and orange juice, showing that they contain glucose. In the cranberry juice, the change in color should be less substantial.

_____

_____

_____

Name_____ Date_____

2. The strip put in the milk without lactase should not change color; after adding lactase, the strip should darken. Students should infer that lactase changed the sugar in the milk to glucose.

_____

_____

3. People who do not have enough lactase in their digestive systems will be able to drink milk without becoming ill if lactase is added to the milk.

_____

_____

INVESTIGATE FURTHER!
EXPERIMENT
Page F55

Make a list of milk products on which you could test the effects of lactase drops.

Some milk products are skim milk, cream, yogurt, cottage cheese, ice cream, butter, sour cream, and yogurt.

Predict how lactase drops will affect these milk products.

Students might predict that the lactase drops will change the milk sugars in these products to glucose.

Record the results of the glucose test for each milk product, before and after adding lactase.

Students should find that none of the milk products contain glucose until after they add lactase.

© Silver Burdett Ginn

CHAPTER
2

Name_____ Date_____

FIBER FINDINGS

Procedure

Write your predictions of foods that are high in fiber.

Some students might predict that whole grains, beans, pasta, and some fruits and vegetables are high in fiber.

_____

_____

In the chart below, **record** the foods you choose for a day's worth of fiber. **Record** the amount of fiber in one serving.

Fiber in a Day	
Food	Amount of Fiber
Students will list various foods given in the tables in their books.	

Record the total number of grams of fiber for the foods you chose.

Students should choose foods that will give a total of 20 g to 35 g of fiber.

CHAPTER
2

ACTIVITY RECORD

Name_____ Date_____

Analyze and Conclude

Write the answers to the questions in your book on lines below.

1. A sample list includes grapes (2 g), oatmeal bread (2 g), lentil soup (5 g), lettuce and tomato sandwich on oatmeal bread (4 g), kidney beans (6 g), brown rice (3 g), corn (2 g), and granola bar (1 g) for a total of 25 g fiber. Students' own diets probably do not contain as much fiber and may not be as balanced as their lists.

_____

2. Students' favorite "good sources of fiber" might include whole wheat tortillas, strawberries, grapes, and carrots. Their favorite foods that are "high in fiber" might include shredded wheat cereal and split pea soup.

_____

_____

_____

3. In general, the low-fiber foods are white bread and highly processed fruits or vegetables that contain a lot of water. High-fiber foods include whole grain breads and cereals; pasta; and fruits or vegetables that are more solid than watery. Students can substitute high-fiber foods for similar low-fiber foods (an orange for grapes, for example).

_____

_____

Name_____ Date_____

UNIT PROJECT LINK

Check the menus you prepared in Chapter 1 to see if they include dietary fiber. In the chart below, list the foods that contain fiber. Next to each food write the amount of fiber in each serving.

Food	Grams of Fiber per Serving

Students can use the tables in their books on pages F56–F57 to find the amount of fiber in some foods. Students can also find out the amount of fiber in foods by reading food labels.

Calculate the amount of fiber that your menus will provide in one day. If the menus don't provide enough fiber—20– 35 g per day—adjust them so they will. In the space below list any substitutions you make in your menus.

Students should give the total amount of fiber that each menu gives in one day. If students need to make adjustments to their menus, they should list the changes they make. In most cases, students will need to substitute a food that is higher in fiber.

_____

_____

_____

Share this information with your group.

Name_____ Date_____

INVESTIGATION 3

1. What could a person do if he or she lacked the enzyme lactase, which breaks down milk sugar to glucose?

They could eat dairy products that are lactose free, or they could supplement their body's supply of lactase by adding it to their food.

2. Describe the stages of digestion that food goes through after it is swallowed. Where are nutrients from digested food absorbed into the blood?

Descriptions should include traveling down the esophagus, breakdown in the stomach, continued breakdown and absorption in the small intestine, waste storage and water absorption in the large intestine, and the passing of waste. Nutrients are absorbed into the blood from the villi that are in the last part of the small intestine.

Tell why it's important to eat a lot of fiber, even though your body can't digest it.

Fiber adds bulk to the waste in the large intestine and holds water, which keeps the waste soft. This makes it easier for the waste to pass from the body.

Name_____ Date_____

HOW THE BODY USES FOOD

What happens at the beginning of digestion?

Digestion begins in the mouth when you bite into food. The teeth cut, tear, grind, and mash the food. The tongue moves the food around the mouth, mashing it and mixing it with saliva. Saliva begins the chemical digestion of food by breaking down starch into sugar. Then the food is swallowed and travels down the esophagus into the stomach.

How can you keep your teeth healthy?

By brushing and flossing after meals and by visiting the dentist for a cleaning at least twice a year

What happens to food after it's swallowed?

Muscles in the esophagus squeeze the food into the stomach where the food mixes with enzymes and acids that break down the food and kill bacteria. From the stomach, partially digested food moves into the small intestine where digestion is finished and nutrients are passed into the bloodstream. Undigested food moves into the large intestine, which stores the waste and absorbs water from it. Eventually, the large intestine moves the waste from the body.

Name_____ Date_____

Think about what you learned in Chapter 2 when you answer the following questions.

1. What did you learn about digestion that helps explain something you've always wondered about?

Answers will vary. Some students might explain that they never really knew what happened to their food once they chewed and swallowed it.

_____

_____

_____

2. What surprised you the most about the digestive system?

Answers will vary. Some students might be surprised at how efficiently the system works.

_____

_____

_____

3. What else would you like to learn about digestion? How could you find out about this?

Answers will vary. Students might suggest reading additional sources or speaking to a dentist or other health care professional.

_____

_____

_____

Name_____ Date_____

UNIT PROJECT WRAP-UP

Think about the menus you made up and the food pyramid supermarket you created for the Unit Project Big Event. Describe what you liked best about this project.

Answers will vary. Some students might have liked preparing the menus best. Others might have liked creating the pyramid.

_____

_____

Compare your group's menus with the menus created by other groups. Describe how your menus are similar to and different from the other groups' menus.

Answers will vary. Students should describe similarities and differences among the menus in the class. Some may share similar foods or the foods are grouped in the same ways.

_____

Tell how planning healthful menus has helped you learn about the nutrients your body needs.

Answers will vary. Students might explain that they have learned which foods contain which nutrients and how much of each nutrient they should have.

_____

_____

How has creating the food pyramid supermarket made you a better food shopper?

Answers will vary. Students might explain that they know how to read food labels and understand what makes a food healthful or what makes it "junk food."

_____

_____